Unplanned Careers: The Working Lives of Middle-Aged Women

Unplanned Careers: The Working Lives of Middle-Aged Women

Edited by
Lois Banfill Shaw
The Ohio State University

LexingtonBooks
D.C. Heath and Company
Lexington, Massachusetts
Toronto

The research for this book was conducted under a contract with the Employment and Training Administration, U.S. Department of Labor, under the authority of the Comprehensive Employment and Training Act. Since researchers undertaking such projects under government sponsorship are encouraged to express their own judgments freely, this study does not represent the Employment and Training Administration's official opinion or policy.

Library of Congress Cataloging in Publication Data

Main entry under title:

Unplanned careers.

Based on interviews made by the National Longitudinal Surveys of Labor Market Experience during the years from 1967 to 1977.
Bibliography: p.
Includes index.
Contents: Introduction and overview/Lois B. Shaw and Theresa O'Brien—Problems of labor market reentry/Lois B. Shaw—Causes of irregular employment patterns/Lois B. Shaw—[etc.]
1. Middle aged women—Employment—United States—Longitudinal studies. I. Shaw, Lois Banfill. II. National Longitudinal Surveys of Labor Market Experience (U.S.)
HD6056.2.U6U56   1982   331.3'94'088042   82-47925
ISBN 0-669-05701-0

Published simultaneously in Canada

Printed in the United States of America

International Standard Book Number: 0-669-05701-0

Library of Congress Catalog Card Number: 82-47925

Contents

Preface and Acknowledgments

In 1967 the Center for Human Resource Research at The Ohio State University initiated the National Longitudinal Survey of the Work Experience of Mature Women under a contract with the Employment and Training Administration of the U.S. Department of Labor. Beginning in the spring of 1967, personal interviews were conducted with a nationally representative sample of over five thousand women who were 30–44 years of age at that time. A short mail survey followed in 1968 and additional personal interviews were conducted in 1969, 1971, 1972, and 1977. Telephone interviews in 1974 and 1976 served to maintain contact with participants and minimize recall problems concerning work experience. Nearly four thousand women remained in the sample in 1977. This book is based on these ten years of interviews. These data are particularly appropriate for studying the changes that have occurred in the lives of middle-aged women in recent years, the subject of this book.

Between 1966 and 1968 the National Longitudinal Surveys (NLS) began interviewing three other groups in addition to the mature women: men who were 45–59 years of age and young women and men in the 14–24 age range. These groups, as well as the mature women, were chosen because they face special labor-market problems. Older men may have problems of health, skill obsolescence, or age discrimination that limit their employment prospects, perhaps forcing early retirement. Young men and women must choose careers and become established in the labor market, and many young women must also decide how to balance work and family roles. Middle-aged women often reenter the labor market after children are in school or grown. All of these problems involve transitions that may best be studied by interviewing the same people over time.

All interviews have been conducted by the U.S. Bureau of the Census and are scheduled to continue through the fifteenth year for each sample. A new survey of 12,000 youths was begun in 1979 with interviews conducted by the National Opinion Research Center of the University of Chicago. The Center for Human Resource Research has the responsibility for preparing interview questions and providing data tapes for public use. The data sets have been widely used by university and government researchers.

While retaining responsibility for opinions expressed and any limitations of the research reported in this book, the authors wish to acknowledge their debt to many individuals who have made this research possible. We especially thank Kezia Sproat whose excellent editorial work has greatly improved the readability of the book and Sherry Stoneman McNamara for her quick and accurate typing of the various drafts of each chapter. Theresa O'Brien, Alice Simon, and Pan-Lang Tsai all devoted many hours to proof-reading and checking the accuracy of tables and figures.

Our research would have been impossible without the expert programming and technical assistance of the center's computer staff. We are especially grateful to Carol Sheets and the late Pat Shannon who created the complex longitudinal data files we used. Pat Shannon, Pam Sparrow, and Helene Churchill were especially helpful in those harried periods when we were approaching project deadlines. We also thank Mary Ann Graessle, Mary Jansen, Rufus Milsted, Michael Motto, Joel Rath, and Steve Strohl for excellent assistance on various chapters.

Among our colleagues at the Department of Labor, we wish to thank Dr. Burt Barnow, who, as director of the Office of Research and Evaluation, has supervised the NLS and encouraged its continuing development. We also thank Dr. Howard Rosen, who initiated these surveys and looked out for their funding and integrity for fifteen years. We thank Ellen Sehgal, the current Labor Department liaison for the surveys, not only for her professional assistance but also as the key individual who has helped smooth the governmental administrative procedures essential to the project. Also, we wish to thank the many Census Bureau personnel who over the years have overseen the entire interviewing process from the training of interviewers to the coding and initial processing of the data. In particular we thank our current liaison person at the Census Bureau, Cheryl Landman. We also appreciate the dedicated efforts of the many census interviewers who have been instrumental in maintaining a remarkably high sample retention rate.

Within the center our special thanks go to Herbert Parnes, who administered the project from the beginning of the surveys until his retirement in 1979, and Michael Borus, the present center director. Their influence in maintaining a collegial atmosphere for the exchange of ideas and advice on research topics has made the center a pleasant and productive work environment. Finally, we are indebted to our colleagues, Jody Crowley, Ron D'Amico, Steve Hills, Choongsoo Kim, Frank Mott, Tom Pollard, Russ Rumberger, and Richard Santos, for reviewing earlier versions of these chapters and providing technical assistance when needed.

1

Introduction and Overview

Lois B. Shaw and
Theresa O'Brien

This book is based on interviews with a nationally representative sample of nearly four thousand women. The National Longitudinal Surveys of Labor Market Experience (NLS) interviewed these women eight times from 1967 to 1977. At the first interview they were 30 to 44 years of age, a range chosen because it represents a transitional stage when many women return to the labor force after staying at home with children. Reinterviews with the same women over these years produced a great deal of valuable data about their problems and successes in becoming reestablished in the labor market.

Before World War II, women typically worked outside the home only before they got married; married women worked, if at all, only in times of family economic crisis or when they became widows. Women who are middle-aged today grew up during the 1940s and 1950s, when the rapid increase in married women's labor-force participation was just beginning. Commonly this generation did not plan for a full working life or even for the return to work after their children were grown. Yet now these women at midlife find themselves in a world of unstable marriages where the need to be self-supporting is thrust on many of them, where a high rate of inflation has increased the cost of rearing and educating their large families, and where the ideal of being a lifelong housewife is widely questioned.

How have they fared, these "women in the middle," the generation caught between the old norms of devotion to family and new ideas about independent and active work lives that many young women aspire to? What problems have they encountered in becoming established in the world of work? How might those who encounter difficulties be helped? These questions are important for social and economic policy because the contributions of these midlife workers bring many families above the poverty line and help others achieve middle-class standards of living. Their labor-market progress between now and retirement will determine whether they can look forward to a reasonably secure and independent old age. Their successes and failures as a transitional generation are also useful indicators of what young women might pursue or avoid in mapping their own careers.

The decade of these interviews was marked by rapid change in societal

The authors thank Alice Simon for her able research assistance.

norms about women's roles, and we recorded not only the women's labor-market experiences but also many other changes in their lives. These include the birth of children or the beginning of the empty-nest stage of the family life cycle, the beginning or ending of marriages, returning to school or participating in job-training programs, health problems in the family, increases or decreases in family income as husbands were promoted or unemployed, and changes in attitudes toward women's roles, both among the women themselves and their husbands. With these data we can provide not only a picture of a particular life-cycle stage at a particular moment in history; we can also discover relationships between the various changes that have occurred in women's lives.

Plan of the Book

This first chapter provides historical background and describes broad changes in the women's family circumstances, attitudes, and employment over the ten years of the interviews. The second chapter focuses on their problems in becoming reestablished in the labor force during the worsening economic climate of the mid-1970s. Because interruptions in employment lead to lower pay and poorer prospects for promotion, it is useful to learn why many women do not work steadily once they reenter the labor force. Chapter 3 investigates women's irregular employment patterns to see if they derive from choice or necessity.

Chapter 4 considers the issue of sex-segregated occupations. As their attachment to the labor force increased, why did so few women move out of poorly paid "women's" jobs? Do women choose stereotypically female occupations because they require less training and less regular employment? Do they choose these jobs because they consider others unfeminine? Is discrimination on the part of employers to blame?

Chapter 5 studies women's rapidly changing attitudes toward their proper roles, the effects of role attitudes on work behavior, and the feedback from work experience to attitudes. It also examines the effects of husbands' attitudes on wives' work activity and wives' work on husbands' subsequent attitudes, using the subsample of women who were married to men in the NLS older men's sample. Also considered is the possibility that men's attitudes toward women's roles may influence the men's own work behavior.

As they grow older, women are increasingly limited in their work activity by health problems. Black women have a particularly high incidence of work-limiting health problems by their late forties and early fifties. Chapter 6 explores in depth how health impairments affect women's work and earnings at midlife.

Female-headed families are the most rapidly growing segment of the population in poverty. Chapter 7 examines work activity and economic status before and after the end of marriage and explores the varied ways that women at midlife cope with the loss of a spouse. Chapter 8 provides a summary of the book.

The Data Set

The original NLS sample of mature women consisted of 5,083 women chosen to be representative of all noninstitutionalized, civilian women age 30–44 in the continental United States at the time of the first interview in 1967. By 1977 approximately four-fifths of the original sample remained; the 2,835 white and 1,072 black women who continued appear to be reasonably representative of their age range in the United States in 1977.[1] Black women were oversampled to provide a large enough number for meaningful analysis. Other races were not oversampled and since only 57 women of other races were interviewed in 1977, they have not been included in the present analysis. Hispanics were not oversampled and are included in the white sample in most cases.

In addition to the mature women's sample, on which this book is based, the NLS conducts longitudinal surveys with four other age-sex groups.[2] We will have occasion to compare today's middle-aged women with their younger counterparts in the NLS young women's sample who were 24–34 years of age in 1978 and with those in the youth sample who were 14–21 when first interviewed in 1979. Some of the women in our sample were married to men who were part of an older men's sample; interviews with these husbands and wives are used in some of the research in this volume.

Contents of the interviews and maintenance of public-use data tapes are the responsibility of the staff of the Center for Human Resource Research at the Ohio State University under a contract with the Employment and Training Administration of the U.S. Department of Labor. Interviews are conducted by the U.S. Bureau of the Census.

Historical Background

Women of the generation in the NLS sample are distinguished from both older and younger women by their large families: they are baby-boom mothers. The oldest women reached their twentieth birthdays during World War II and most began childbearing soon after. The youngest reached age 20 at the peak of the baby boom in the late 1950s. Yet these same women have also worked outside the home to a greater extent than any previous generation. They are the first generation whose entire adulthood followed the abrupt change in married women's working lives brought about by the need for women workers during World War II. Prior to this time, white women often worked before marriage but seldom after unless they were widowed or divorced. Black women were much more likely to work than their white counterparts. Since the historical experience of white and black women differs markedly, we consider each in turn.

White Women

Our sample is a transitional generation between those who followed the old norm that working outside of the home after marriage was exceptional, and present-day young women, who will work outside the home for a substantial part of their adult lives. Prewar and postwar work patterns are illustrated in figure 1–1, which compares the labor-force participation of married women approximately the ages of the oldest and youngest third of the NLS sample with those of their mothers' generation, who are about twenty-five years older.[3] Before World War II, participation rates were low and increased very little beyond the childrearing years. Although the mothers of the women in our sample stayed at home and most of the NLS women themselves returned to work after childrearing, over half of their married daughters were working in their twenties; that is, at the age at which traditionally women left the labor force.

Only a quarter of white women in the NLS sample had the example of a working mother during their teenage years. The older women in the sample had few role models of married women working at desirable jobs since their were widespread rules against employing married women as teachers and clerical workers throughout the 1930s. A survey of urban school districts in 1941 found that 87 percent did not hire married women. Many companies also had policies of hiring only single women as clerical workers (Oppenheimer 1970, pp. 127–134).

The younger women of the sample, who grew up during and after World War II, had more potential role models of employed married women. Nevertheless, these women were teenagers or young adults in the postwar years when traditional roles were strongly encouraged: popular magazines extolled the housewife who devoted herself solely to the needs of her husband and children, and employed women were depicted as neurotic and unfeminine.[4] Although the trend toward more married women working continued throughout the 1950s in spite of this hostile climate of opinion, popular views probably influenced women's plans for their future roles. In fact, as late as 1968 only 27 percent of the 14–24 year olds in the NLS young women's sample had definite plans for working at age 35, but by 1979, when the oldest had reached that age, 60 percent were in fact in the

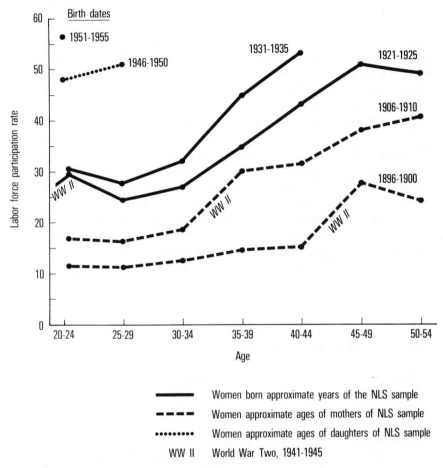

Source: Adapted from Robinson (1980), table 5.

Figure 1–1. Labor-Force Participation Rate by Age for Married Women
Born at Selected Dates

labor force (Shapiro 1980; U.S. Department of Labor 1979). Only recently have many young women begun to plan ahead for their working years: in the 1979 NLS survey of youth about two-thirds of these young women had occupational plans for age 35 (Shapiro and Crowley 1981).

Because they were young adults before the return to work after child-bearing became a well-established norm, many middle-aged women were not prepared for the world of work. Many had to replan their lives after their children no longer occupied all of their time or upon being widowed or divorced.[5]

Black Women

When they were 15 years old, slightly over half of black women in this generation had mothers who worked outside the home.[6] Nearly half of the sample grew up in the rural South; if their mothers worked they were farm workers or, less frequently, private household workers. Among women who lived in urban areas, over half of those whose mothers worked reported their mother's occupation as private household worker. So nearly three-quarters of the working mothers of black women were employed in farming or housework. During World War II, opportunities for black women outside these two occupations increased to a modest degree, and the labor-force participation of black women aged 20–49 increased from about 50 percent to 55 percent (Robinson 1980). Among women who were teenagers in urban areas during the war years, about 25 percent had working mothers who held blue-collar jobs, up from about 16 percent reported by older women whose mothers had worked before World War II.

During the 1950s as well as the war years, large numbers of black families moved out of the rural South. In 1940 over half of the black population was rural and Southern, but by 1960 only one-quarter was (Farley 1970, p. 50). Because of this migration the younger black women in the NLS sample were less likely than their older counterparts to have mothers employed in agriculture but even more likely to have mothers who were employed as domestics. As they moved to urban areas, about one-quarter of working mothers were employed as blue-collar or service workers; rarely were they in white-collar occupations (less than 10 percent). Thus, unlike white women, whose mothers usually did not work outside the home, black women frequently had such role models, but their models worked in low-wage unskilled occupations. Even if today's middle-aged black women could have foreseen future opportunities in white-collar jobs and better paying blue-collar jobs, the poor education available in the rural South and the high level of poverty in both North and South would have prevented many of them from preparing to take advantage of these opportunities.

This historical background is crucial to an understanding of the work behavior of today's middle-aged women. In the remainder of this book we will see how both black and white women have coped with their new, often unplanned work roles.

Economic and Social Changes, 1967–1977

The 1967–1972 years were a time of prosperity with relatively mild inflation: for several years in the late 1960s, unemployment rates were historically low—consistently below 4 percent. In the early 1970s, unemployment increased moderately, to between 5 and 6 percent. The 1972–1977 period began in reasonable prosperity but ended with high unemployment and inflation: the average increase in the consumer price index was nearly 9 percent per year over the period, and 1975 brought the worst recession the nation had suffered since World War II. At the time of the NLS tenth-year interview in 1977, the overall unemployment rate was about 7 percent (U.S. Department of Labor 1980, pp. 253, 384).

Along with these general economic trends, over the 1967–1972 period real family income of the women in the NLS sample increased by about 17 percent for whites and 25 percent for blacks. Although these increases came partly from the greater contribution of the women themselves, increases in income from husband's earnings and other sources were also quite large, about 15 percent for white and 20 percent for black families.[7] The 1972–1977 period, however, showed little further change in real income: white family income grew about 4 percent and black family income declined 3 percent.

Since the late 1960s, women's roles and rights in society have been the subject of much debate, and changing views about women's roles are reflected in the attitudes of women in the NLS sample. In 1967 well over 90 percent thought it was all right for a woman with school-age children to work if it was necessary to make ends meet and about 75 percent thought that such a woman should work if she wanted to and her husband agreed. However, in 1967 very few approved of women working if the husband disapproved. Figure 1–2 shows how these views changed over the ten survey years. While support for working if necessary remained constant and almost universal, support for working in the other two situations increased considerably, so that by 1977 nearly one-third of the women thought that a woman should work if she wanted to, even if her husband disagreed with her decision.

The 1972 and 1977 interviews included nine additional questions on women's roles. Changes favorable to women's greater involvement outside the home were found in virtually every case. The largest change was in the percentage of women who agreed that a woman's place is in the home. In 1967, 45 percent of white women and 48 percent of black women held this view, but by 1977 the percentage agreeing had dropped to 32 for white women and 37 for black.[8] Attitudes on the question of whether working wives contribute to juvenile delinquency showed the least change of any of the questions asked. Over 40 percent of both whites and blacks linked women's working with children's delinquency in both years. Apparently the fear of delinquency if children are left unsupervised causes considerable concern among a substantial minority of the population even when their other beliefs about women's roles are changing rapidly.

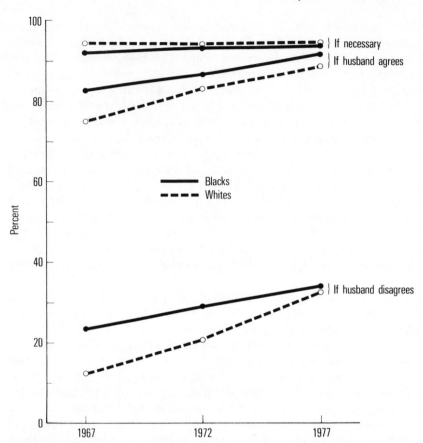

Note: The question asked whether it is all right for a married woman with children between the ages of 6 and 12 to work under three circumstances: if it is absolutely necessary to make ends meet; if she wants to and her husband agrees; if she wants to even if her husband doesn't particularly like it.

Figure 1-2. Attitudes toward Married Women Working: Percentage of Women Who Agree that It Is All Right for a Woman to Work

Changes in Family Responsibilities

During the ten years since they were first interviewed, family circumstances changed for many women. Some changed marital status and some had additional children, but the majority entered a stage of decreasing family responsibilities as their children grew older and in some cases left home. Fewer women were married and living with their husbands in 1977 than in

1967, and the percentage who were widowed, divorced, or separated had increased from 8 to 15 percent for white women and from 27 to 38 percent for black women. A small number were married for the first time during the decade; in 1977 only 4 percent of white women and 5 percent of black women had never married.

The marital status differences between white and black women in their middle years are striking and should be kept in mind when comparisons of the two groups are made. About three-fourths of white women but less than half of black women were married to the same husband throughout the period (figure 1-3). Only 4 percent of white women were widowed, separated, or divorced for the entire ten years, but 20 percent of black women had been the sole family head throughout this period. An additional 18 percent of black women had ended their marriages during the period and had not remarried by 1977. Over 80 percent of white women but less than 60 percent of black women were married in 1977.

In 1967 over 40 percent of the married women had preschool children, but ten years later the percentage was less than 5 (table 1-1). Correspondingly, 11 percent of white and 18 percent of black married women had no children under 18 in 1967, but by 1977 over 40 percent of all married women had reached this stage in the family life cycle. About 30 percent had no children at home in 1977; about 10 percent had children 18 and over who still lived at home. Between 1967 and 1977, the average number of children at home declined from 2.8 to 1.7 for white women and from 3.5 to 2.1 for black women. Unmarried women were also less likely to have children under 18 in 1977 than in 1967: the percentage of unmarried women with children dropped from approximately one-half to one-third for white women and from three-quarters to one-half for black women.

Figure 1-4 shows further details on the declining percentage of women with preschool children for different groups of women. As expected, the largest decline occurred for women who were 30–34 in 1967. Over 55 percent of these women had preschool children in 1967, but ten years later when they were age 40–44, fewer than 10 percent still had preschool children at home. Notice that each successive cohort had fewer preschool children over the years. For example, the percentage of women who had preschool children at age 35–39 fell from 38 percent in 1967 to 28 percent in 1972. The women who were 35–39 in 1972 did not have smaller families than older women had; instead, the observed trend toward fewer preschool children is entirely accounted for by a trend toward earlier childbearing. Although completed family size was almost identical for the three groups, 3.1 children for the oldest group and 3.2 for the other two, the average woman age 50–54 in 1977 had her youngest child at age 31 while the average woman of 40–44 had her last child at age 29.[9] Because the younger cohorts tended to have their children when they themselves were younger, they were freed

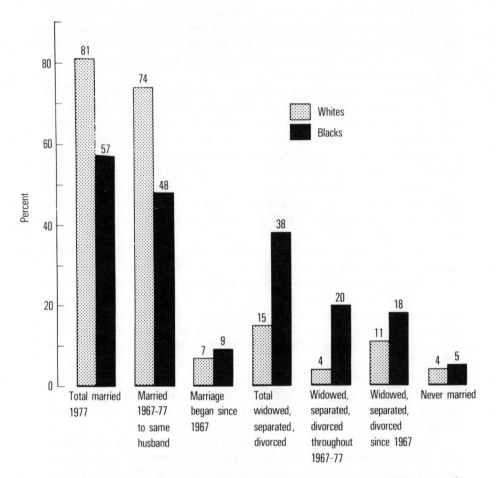

Figure 1–3. Percentage Distribution of Women by 1977 Marital Status and Whether Current Status Began Since 1967

from preschool childcare responsibilities sooner in their life cycles than were the older cohorts: thus the tendency toward more youthful childbearing accounts for some of the observed increase in women's labor-force participation. In addition, involvement in work outside the home was facilitated for all cohorts as they and their children grew older and the children entered school.

Table 1-1
Age of Youngest Child and Number of Children at Home in 1967 and 1977,
by Current Marital Status
(percentage distributions)

Age of Youngest Child	Married		Not Married[a]	
	1967	*1977*	*1967*	*1977*
Whites				
0–5	41	4	13	[b]
6–17	48	52	38	33
None under 18	11	44	49	66
Total percent	100	100	100	100
Sample size	2,478	2,298	357	535
Mean number of children at home	2.8	1.7	1.4	0.9
Blacks				
0–5	44	4	33	4
6–17	38	52	44	45
None under 18	18	44	23	51
Total percent	100	100	100	100
Sample size	691	586	381	484
Mean number of children at home	3.5	2.1	2.9	2.0

[a]Includes widowed, separated, divorced, and never married.
[b]Less than .5 percent.

Work Experience

Labor-Force Participation

As family responsibilities decreased and societal attitudes toward women working outside the home became more supportive, the labor-force participation rate of white women in the sample increased from slightly over 45 to nearly 60 percent. However, the labor-force participation of black women, already over 65 percent at the first interview, declined slightly to about 62 percent by 1977.[10]

As figure 1–5 shows, the labor-force participation of the younger women of both races increased throughout the 1967–1977 period. At the

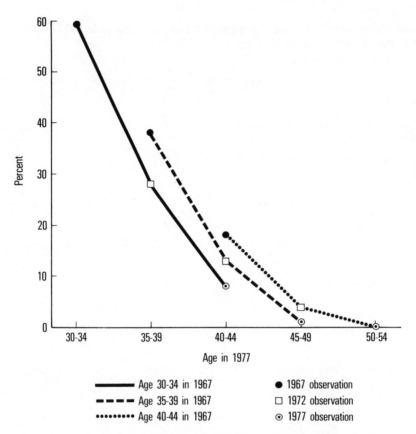

Figure 1-4. Percentage of Women with Preschool Children in 1967, 1972, and 1977, by Women's Ages

older end of the age spectrum, the percentage of black women who were working declined throughout the period, whereas for white women a modest decline began only after 1972.

The labor-force participation of white women has been increasing in each age range. For example, the oldest women, who were age 40–44 in 1967, had a labor-force participation rate of slightly less than 50 percent in that year, but the youngest, who reached their early forties in 1977, had a participation rate of over 60 percent. These trends occurred before birth rates began to decline, but as previously noted, the youngest women in the sample had their children at younger ages and hence were less likely to have young children when they reached their early forties. For black women, no consistent trend can be seen over the ten-year period.

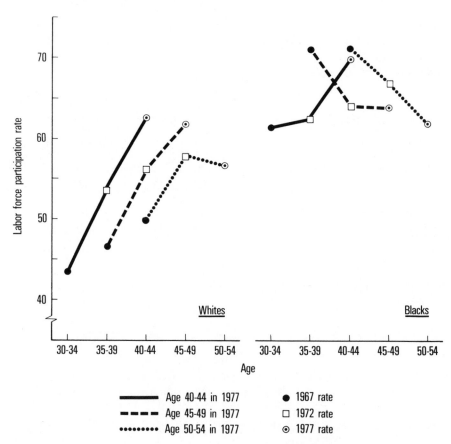

Figure 1-5. Labor-Force Participation Rate in 1967, 1972, and 1977, by Age

Work Patterns

The vast majority of women in the NLS sample worked outside the home at some time during the eleven years for which work-history data are available.[11] As table 1-2 shows, only 16 percent of white women and 9 percent of black women never worked at all. However, some women have worked very little. The white sample is split fairly equally into a third who worked very little or not at all, a third who worked a moderate amount (25–74 percent of the weeks), and a third who worked fairly continuously (at least 75 percent of the weeks). Even among women in long-term marriages, the housewife who never works is a decided minority. On the other

Table 1-2
Percentage of Weeks Worked 1966-1977, by 1977 Marital Status and When Status Began
(percentage distributions)

			Percentage of Weeks Worked				
Marital Status	*0*	*1-24*	*25-49*	*50-74*	*75 or More*	*Total Percent*	*Sample Size*
Whites							
Total[a]	16	18	16	17	33	100	2,835
Married 1967-1977 to same husband	19	20	17	16	28	100	2,105
Other	8	11	14	18	49	100	724
Blacks							
Total	9	16	13	18	44	100	1,071
Married 1967-1977 to same husband	8	17	14	18	43	100	491
Other	9	15	13	17	46	100	567

[a]Total includes a few women who could not be classified by marital status in all years.

hand, less than 30 percent of white married women worked continuously. Women who were not married during part or all of the period were, of course, much more likely to be strongly attached to the labor force—nearly half of them had worked for most of the eleven years.

Nearly 45 percent of black women had worked most of the eleven years while about a quarter worked little or not at all. In contrast to white women, the work patterns of black women in long-term marriages differed very little from those who were not married during all or part of the period.

Table 1-3 shows the timing as well as the amount of the women's work over the eleven years. About 60 percent of the black women and 45 percent of the white were working in both the first and last year of the interviews.[12] More white women entered than left the labor force, but for black women the reverse was true. About 15 percent of the women who were working at both the beginning and end of the period had nevertheless worked less than 75 percent of the time; they either worked regularly only part of the year or, more commonly, they spent a considerable period out of the labor force during the ten years. Similarly, some women worked at some time during the period but not at the beginning or end. Counting these two groups of sporadic workers, we see that about 20 percent of the women had irregular work histories; another 5 to 10 percent entered or left employment and did

Table 1-3
Whether Respondent Worked in 1967 and 1977, by Percentage of Weeks Worked 1966-1977

Percentage of Weeks Worked	Worked Neither	Worked 1967 Only	Worked 1977 Only	Worked Both	Total Percent[a]
Whites					
0	16	—	—	—	16
1-74	8	10	19	13	50
75 or more	—	1	1	31	33
Total	24	11	20	44	100
Blacks					
0	9	—	—	—	9
1-74	5	17	8	17	47
75 or more	—	1	1	42	44
Total	14	18	9	59	100

[a]Total sample sizes are 2,835 whites and 1,071 blacks.

not work steadily after entering or before leaving, so the total of sporadic workers over the ten years is in the range of 25-30 percent.

Table 1-4 shows the differing degrees of work involvement of women at different stages in the childrearing cycle. White women returned to work in the greatest numbers during the years when their children were attending school; 30 percent of women whose youngest child was between 10 and 17 years old in 1977 had entered employment during the previous ten years. Not so many enter before the youngest child goes to school or after this child leaves school, but we observe a net flow into the labor force as long as there are children at home. Surprisingly, during the empty-nest stage when they are popularly believed to return to work, more women left than returned to employment. However, over 40 percent of white women without children at home worked steadily over the eleven years. More black women left than entered the work force, whatever their childrearing responsibilities. However, about half of black women who either had no children or only grown children worked throughout most of the eleven years of the interviews.

Full-time or Part-time Work

The percentage of women who worked full-time (thirty-five hours a week or more) varied considerably among women with differing patterns of work

Table 1-4
Whether Respondent Worked in 1967 and 1977 and Percentage of Weeks Worked 1966–1977, by Age of Youngest Child
(percentage distributions)

Age of Youngest Child at Home in 1977	Worked Neither		Worked 1967 Only	Worked 1977 Only	Worked Both		Total Percent	Sample Size
	0	1–74			Less than 75 Percent	75 Percent or More		
Whites								
Total	16	8	11	20	13	31	100	2,835
0–9	27	10	13	19	16	15	100	329
10–17	18	10	7	30	15	21	100	1,112
18 and over	13	7	12	18	11	40	100	506
None	12	6	16	10	12	44	100	888
Blacks								
Total	9	5	18	9	17	42	100	1,072
0–9	13	10	23	13	17	24	100	170
10–17	10	5	18	14	17	36	100	403
18 and over	5	5	15	4	13	58	100	202
None	7	3	17	5	20	48	100	297

attachment (figure 1-6). Women who worked continuously usually worked full-time as well: of the women with the most continuous work records—those working at both the beginning and end of the period who worked at least 75 percent of the weeks between—over 80 percent were full-time workers in 1967 and over 85 percent in 1977. In contrast, a much smaller percentage of women who left after 1967 had been full-time workers in 1967. An even bigger gap separates the continuous workers from the new entrants in 1977. Only 56 percent of white entrants and 62 percent of black were full-time workers. Women who worked in both 1967 and 1977 but less than 75 percent of the weeks between had only slightly higher percentages of full-time work than new entrants. Part-time workers are concentrated among labor-market entrants and women who work irregularly. Continuous part-time work is uncommon.

Progress and Problems

Education and Training

Educational attainment is an important determinant of labor-market success. When they were young, many middle-aged women did not have the educational opportunities that are taken for granted today. Well over half of black women and fully 30 percent of white had not completed high school by 1977; only 10 percent of white women and 8 percent of black were college graduates (figure 1-7).

Over the decade of the interviews, many women returned to school: 7 percent of white women and 10 percent of black completed at least one additional year of school (table 1-5). Although some completed high school at this time, most of the gains in educational attainment were at the college level or above. The percentage of women with some college education increased from 19 to 21 percent for whites and from 9 to 14 percent for blacks, while the percentage with some graduate-school education doubled for whites (from 1.5 to 3 percent) and rose by 60 percent for blacks (from 3 to 5 percent). These latter figures indicate that over one-third of the black women and over one-half of the white women who had attended graduate school by 1977 had reached this educational level since the first interview; that is, after they were 30 years old.

In addition to completing more schooling, large numbers of mature women reported participating in and completing other educational or training programs and actually using their new skills on their jobs between 1967 and 1977.[13] Nearly one-fifth of the sample completed some kind of job training during that time. Women with at least some college are not only most likely to attain more education, but also most likely to get job train-

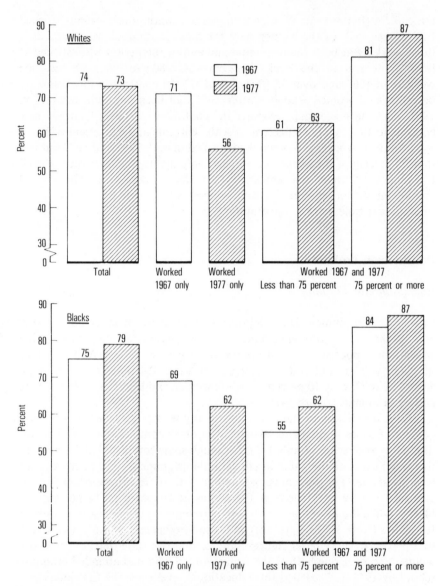

Figure 1-6. Percentage of Wage and Salary Workers Who Worked Full
Time in 1967 and 1977 by Whether Respondent Worked in
1967 and 1977, and Percentage of Weeks Worked between
1966 and 1977

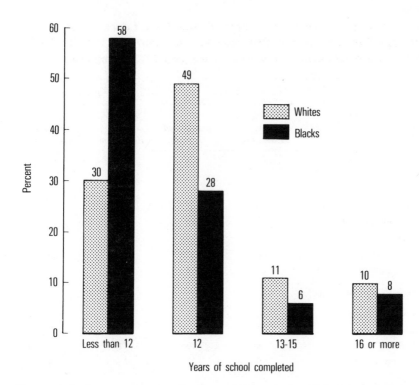

Figure 1–7. Percentage Distribution of Women by 1977 Educational Attainment

ing (table 1–5). Particularly striking are the black college graduates, three-fourths of whom took job training.

Women who exhibited relatively strong attachments to the labor force during the ten years were also much more likely to receive more education or job training than average. Women who entered or stayed in the labor force during the decade sought more job training than those who worked little or left the labor force, as evidenced by the larger percentages of training participants among the "Worked both years" and "Worked 1977 only" categories than among the "Worked neither year" or "Worked 1967 only" categories in table 1–5.

Teachers and nurses frequently must return to school to maintain their certificates. Many professional and managerial occupations demand a higher level of education or training to obtain or sustain a position. Women in these occupations in 1977 had the highest rates of participation in education and training (table 1–5).[14] In addition, white-collar workers and skilled

Table 1-5
**Percentages of Women Who Completed Additional Education or
Participated in Job-Training Programs between 1967 and 1977, by 1967
Educational Attainment, Work Experience, and 1977 Occupation**

	Whites		Blacks	
Characteristic	*Completed More Education*	*Participated in Training*	*Completed More Education*	*Participated in Training*
Total	7	18	10	17
1967 Education				
Less than high school	3	4	5	4
High school dropout	10	12	12	13
High school graduate	3	18	6	22
Attended college	16	24	33	16
College graduate or above	21	38	26	76
Whether Respondent Worked				
Worked neither year	4	1	1	2
Worked 1967 only	3	8	7	7
Worked 1977 only	8	19	11	18
Worked both years	10	29	13	24
1977 Occupation				
Teachers	44	54	41	72
Nurses	19	64	a	a
Other professional	23	46	31	47
Managerial	13	40	a	a
Clerical and sales	6	24	18	34
Crafts	0	34	a	a
Service	5	20	11	17
Other[b]	2	5	5	5

[a]Percentages not shown when sample size less than 20.
[b]Includes operatives and farm workers.

craftswomen received more training over the decade than those in service
and other occupations. Whether they were strongly attached to the labor
force or in relatively good occupations, those in favorable labor-market
positions acquired additional education or job training more often than
those in less favorable positions.

Wages

The average woman who was employed in 1977 was working at a somewhat higher wage than the average woman worker in 1967. (All wages are in constant 1977 dollars.) Although white women were making only 6 percent more per hour, black women were making 20 percent more (figure 1-8). However, these averages include women who were not working at both dates—that is, women who left or entered employment during the period—and, therefore, do not reflect the experience of women with fairly continuous work experience. White women who were working in both 1967 and 1977 experienced real-wage increases of 13 percent if they worked fairly continuously throughout the period. Women who worked less regularly had virtually no increase in real wages on average. Black women who worked steadily had wage increases that averaged about 17 percent, while less regular workers had increases of 11 percent. Both black and white women who entered the labor force after 1967 had wages close to those of other intermittent workers. The one exception was white women who entered early enough to have worked for 75 percent of the period—these women's wages resembled those of other continuous workers.

The wages of all black women working in 1977 were 20 percent higher than those of all black women working in 1967. While women who were working at both dates made substantial wage gains, another reason for the overall increase in average wages between the two dates was that many low-wage workers dropped out of the labor force and were replaced by new entrants with somewhat higher wages. Thus some black middle-aged women were making progress toward better jobs, but others with poor jobs were leaving the labor force. The importance of steady employment is apparent for both black and white women.

Occupations

Occupational changes over the decade of the interviews largely parallel the changes in wages, as shown in table 1-6. Women who worked steadily were more likely to move into professional or managerial jobs than were other groups. Thirty percent of white and nearly a quarter of black women with a strong work attachment were professional or managerial workers by 1977. Changes were smaller for intermittent workers.

One cause of the observed wage increases for black workers, even those who worked irregularly, was probably their movement out of private household employment. The occupational difference between black women who left and those who entered the labor force is striking. Almost one-third of the black women who left the labor force by 1977 had been household

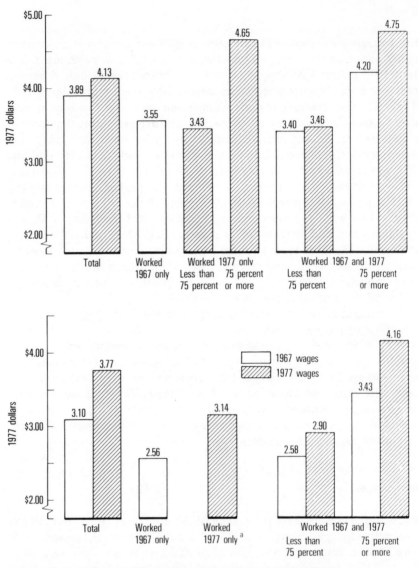

^aSample size insufficient to allow for percent of weeks worked breakdown.

Figure 1–8. Average Hourly Earnings of Wage and Salary Workers in 1967 and 1977 by Whether Respondent Worked in 1967 and 1977, and Percentage of Weeks Worked between 1966 and 1977

Table 1-6
Occupation in 1967 and 1977, by Whether Respondent Worked in 1967 and 1977 and Percentage of Weeks Worked between 1966 and 1977
(percentage distributions)

| | All Workers | | Worked 1967 Only | Worked 1977 Only | Worked Both | | | |
| | | | | | Less than 75 Percent | | 75 Percent or More | |
Occupation	1967	1977			1967	1977	1967	1977
Whites								
Professional, managerial	20	25	15	19	17	20	23	30
Clerical, sales	42	42	37	46	41	42	44	40
Blue collar[a]	19	14	23	10	18	16	17	16
Private household	2	2	4	3	3	3	1	1
Other service	14	15	15	18	18	17	12	12
Farm[b]	3	2	5	3	3	3	3	1
Total sample	100	100	100	100	100	100	100	100
Sample size	1,578	1,798	333	559	373	368	873	871
Blacks								
Professional, managerial	11	18	4	13	1	5	18	24
Clerical, sales	13	17	9	24	9	11	17	18
Blue collar[a]	20	18	17	17	15	12	23	21
Private household	23	14	32	12	34	24	16	10
Other service	28	31	28	32	30	41	27	26
Farm[b]	5	2	10	1	11	7	1	1
Total percent	100	100	100	100	100	100	100	100
Sample size	811	697	208	102	190	186	413	409

[a]Includes craftsmen, operatives, and laborers.
[b]Includes farmers, farm managers, and farm laborers.

workers in 1967; an additional 10 percent were farm workers. In contrast, only 13 percent of the new entrants were in these two poorly paid occupations. Only 13 percent of the job leavers were white-collar workers, but 37 percent of the entrants held white-collar jobs. The overall changes in the kinds of occupations that black women hold represent some real progress. The observed wage gains also are due partly to the replacement of workers with low skills, usually older women, by younger women who are more likely to qualify for white-collar jobs or to find regular service work that is better paid than private household employment.

Unemployment

For some women who want to work, unemployment is a problem, and for women who are the sole support of themselves and their families, it is not a trivial problem. Figure 1-9 shows the percentage of women with any labor force attachment who experienced any unemployment in the year preceding each of six interviews.[15] The unemployment experience of women in our sample only partially mirrors national averages. In particular, although all groups experienced an increase in unemployment in the year preceding the 1976 interview (which includes six or seven months of the severe 1975 recession period), only among unmarried black women was this an exceptionally poor year.[16] Indeed, over 20 percent of these women were unemployed at some time during the year, and over 10 percent were unemployed for three or more months. Clearly the 1975 recession strongly affected the prospects of the very women who were least likely to have other resources to tide them over a period when they could not find work. In contrast, married black women had generally lessening prospects of becoming unemployed over the ten-year period, and their unemployment rates showed convergence with those of white unmarried women. Within both races, women who were not married had consistently higher probabilities of becoming unemployed than did married women.

Women's Contribution to Family Income

The slower growth of family income during 1972-1977 than during 1967-1972 is shown in table 1-7. For white married couples the overall growth in income from 1967 to 1972 reflected increases in husband's earnings and other income, increases in the wife's earnings, and increases in the percentage of families with working women. A slowing down of the growth in all of these components occurred in 1972-1977. Over the ten years, white working women's contribution to family income remained constant at

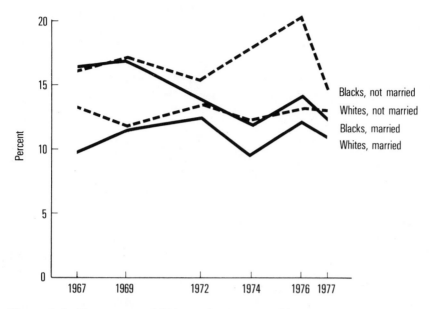

Figure 1-9. Percentage of Women in the Labor Force Who Experienced Any Unemployment during the Previous Year, by Current Marital Status and Race

about 28 percent of the total.[17] By 1977 about 60 percent of middle-aged couples depended on the wife's earnings to some extent.

Black married couples' incomes increased by over 25 percent between 1967 and 1972 and were virtually constant between 1972 and 1977. In the first five years, increases in the earnings of both husbands and wives were offset only slightly by the decline in the percentage of families with working wives. In the second five years, fewer wives were working and on balance earnings and other income of both husbands and wives failed to increase. The worsening economic climate of these years evidently hurt black families more than white: the major contribution that working wives make to the welfare of many black families is evident, even when many of them are working at very low-paying jobs. In 1977, 65 percent of black husband-wife families had working wives, who on average contributed 37 percent of family income.

Most women who are not married must, of course, support themselves and their families to a large degree. In 1977 their own earnings amounted to about three-quarters of white women's total income and over two-thirds of black women's income (table 1-7). For these women the main sources of income other than their own earnings are earnings of children, child-support

Table 1-7
Average Total Family Income with and without Women's Earnings
(1977 dollars)

Year	Total Income, All Families	Total Income, Families without Working Women	Families with Working Women					Sample Size
			Total Income	Women's Earnings	Other Income	Women's Earnings as Percent of Total	Percent of Families with Working Women	
Whites			**Husband-Wife Families**					
1967	18,500	17,200	19,900	5,500	14,400	28	48	1,967
1972	22,300	20,400	23,800	6,400	17,400	27	58	1,531
1977	23,700	21,200	25,500	7,000	18,500	28	59	1,323
Blacks								
1967	12,400	10,000	13,300	4,400	8,900	33	71	577
1972	15,900	12,100	17,500	6,700	10,800	38	68	427
1977	15,800	11,800	17,800	6,500	11,300	37	65	327
Whites			**Female-Headed Families**[a]					
1967	10,100	5,500	11,400	7,900	3,500	69	78	298
1972	11,300	6,400	12,700	8,800	3,900	69	77	334
1977	11,100	5,900	12,800	9,500	3,300	74	76	344
Blacks								
1967	5,900	4,300	6,300	4,500	1,800	71	73	335
1972	8,000	6,100	9,000	6,000	3,000	67	64	344
1977	8,300	5,500	9,700	6,600	3,100	68	64	338

Note: Women's earnings refers to earnings of the respondents in the sample.

[a]Female-headed families include all women who are widowed, separated, divorced or never married at each date. The term female-headed family is used here for its brevity. Women living alone and in a few cases women living with male relatives are included, and hence the group described differs from the official Census definition of female-headed families.

payments, social security dependents' allowances (for widows), and welfare. Income from these sources increased during the 1967–1972 period and then declined in 1972–1977. This decline probably represented not so much the worsening economic environment as a decline in all of these support possibilities as children grew up.

Comparing 1972 and 1977, white female-headed households in which the woman herself worked had higher average earnings in the latter year that offset the smaller amounts of income from other sources. In the 24 percent of female-headed families in which the women did not work, income was considerable lower in 1977 than in 1972. If these women had children, they were quite likely to be living below the poverty line.

Black female heads of households who were working were somewhat better off in 1977 than in 1972. However, the 36 percent who did not work had smaller incomes in 1977 than in 1972. Unemployment, low levels of education, and poor health are particularly serious problems for this group. Discrimination in the labor market because of race, sex, or age may have added to their disabilities. All of these factors may have contributed to a lower level of self-support among black unmarried women.

The importance of women's earnings to their families and to society can be demonstrated in another way. Table 1–8 shows the percentage of families whose incomes would fall below the poverty line without the earnings of the wife or female family head, compared with the actual percentage

Table 1–8
Percentage of Families in Poverty and Percentage that Would Be in Poverty without Women's Earnings, by Current Marital Status

Year	Whites		Blacks	
	Without Respondent's Earnings	*With Respondent's Earnings*	*Without Respondent's Earnings*	*With Respondent's Earnings*
Married				
1967	9	6	43	32
1972	7	4	33	21
1977	6	4	25	16
Not married				
1967	75	26	93	62
1972	74	23	83	53
1977	67	18	73	41

Note: *Poverty* is defined by total family income being below the poverty line for families of different sizes, per the official guidelines published yearly in *Current Population Reports*, Series P-60. Sample sizes as shown in table 1–7.

that are poor when these earnings are included.[18] Even among white married couples, the group with the lowest incidence of poverty, about 50 percent more families would be poor if wives did not work. In 1977 the poverty rate among black husband-wife families was cut from about one-quarter to one-sixth by the contribution of wives.

The vast majority of unmarried women would be poor if they did not work: in 1977 this held true for two-thirds of white and three-quarters of black unmarried women. White women more commonly than black had earnings high enough to have incomes above the poverty line, yet 18 percent were poor in 1977. Some of the factors that made earning an adequate income difficult for black women have been discussed already. In addition, black unmarried women had heavier family responsibilities than white: in 1977 on average blacks had two children at home as compared with one for white women. Even with children leaving home and increasing levels of income, over 40 percent of black women who head families were poor. As they grow older they may become even more vulnerable to health problems, and, in recessions, to unemployment.

Summary

The ten-year period 1967–1977 brought significant changes in the lives of women in their middle years. Most were entering a stage of increasing freedom from family responsibilities; some had lost husbands; many no longer had children at home. For our cohort, these events occurred during ten years that began in prosperity and ended with high rates of both inflation and unemployment, accompanied by a slowing down of the growth in family income. The period observed here also brought widespread questioning of traditional roles for women. These events accompanied increasing labor-force participation by most white women, but some decline in the participation of black women, especially those in their late forties and early fifties.

During the ten-year period, over 80 percent of white women and 90 percent of black women worked at some time. Patterns of work behavior varied. Many younger women reentered the work force while some of the older women were leaving paid employment. About 35 percent of white women and 45 percent of black worked fairly continuously througout the ten years. However, sporadic work patterns were also common. Women who worked continuously over the decade had real-wage gains of about 15 percent. However, women who reentered the labor force or worked sporadically were no better off in 1977 than the average female worker in 1967.

The growing employment of women is important for their families and society. The percentage of families in poverty was reduced by at least 50 percent because of the contribution of working wives. Households headed by women, a growing percentage as the women move into their fifties, have extremely high probabilities of being poor unless the women themselves can find adequately paid employment. White women who are now middle-aged were generally socialized to believe that home and family would provide a lifelong career: for many women this belief has proven unrealistic. Some have undertaken additional education, and many work steadily at good jobs. Others may need training programs geared to their particular needs if they are to become self-supporting.

As a group, unmarried black women are the most disadvantaged of women at midlife. Many had poor educational and job opportunities when they were younger. They suffered much more unemployment than any other group during the 1975 recession, and 40 percent of them were poor in 1977. Especially after age 45, many were beginning to leave the labor market. The future does not look bright for these women unless more of them can receive additional job training or adequate income maintenance.

Notes

1. Attrition is accounted for by 3 percent who have died, 4 percent who could not be located, and 15 percent who refused to be interviewed. Among black women, attrition was heavier in the North than in the South. For both races, women with children at home were slightly more likely to remain in the sample than those without children. Biases due to attrition have been partially corrected by reweighting the sample. The weights used in the tabular analyses are based on the probability that a woman will be included in the sample in 1977. See Center for Human Resource Research (1981) for a more complete description of the sampling weights.

2. A complete description of the NLS may be found in Center for Human Resource Research (1981).

3. Labor-force participation rates are taken from the historical series constructed by Robinson (1980) and are used with his permission. Women in the NLS sample were born from April 1922 through March 1937. These figures are for all married women. Since white women are nine-tenth of the total, their labor-force participation is overstated only slightly.

4. A good discussion of the popular writing of the period is contained in Chafe (1972, chapter 9). The view that women who aspired to any role other than housewife were neurotic was propounded by both psychiatrists and journalists (see, for example, Deutsch 1944; Lundberg and Farnham 1947).

5. Rubin (1979), in her interviews with middle-aged women, repeatedly notes the lack of preparation for the period after children leave home.

6. All data on mother's occupation are tabulated from questions asked about the occupation of the mother when the respondent was 15 years old. Tabulations include only women who lived with their mothers at that age.

7. Total family income and women's contributions are discussed in more detail later in the chapter. For both races, increases in the number of women without husbands caused decreases in average income growth.

8. Although older women have somewhat more traditional attitudes than younger women on this question, the differences are not large within the age range of our sample, and all age groups shared in the trend away from traditional attitudes. However, much younger women have less traditional attitudes. In 1979, only 15 percent of young women 14–21 agreed that a woman's place is in the home. (This percentage was tabulated from the NLS youth survey.)

9. The youngest will have a small number of children after age 40, but, at most, average completed family size will probably not increase by more than another one-tenth of a child.

10. NLS labor-force participation figures are consistently slightly higher than those published by the Current Population Survey (CPS). Borus, Mott, and Nestel (1978) attribute these differences primarily to the fact that CPS responses are not always self-reported.

11. In the first interview in 1967, weeks worked in the previous year were ascertained. Thus the work history covers an eleven-year period from 1966 to 1977. However, there are two years, 1973 and 1975, in which work histories were not asked. In all cases we have assumed that the nine years observed are representative of the full eleven years. At a time of increasing labor-force participation, we may be slightly understating work attachment.

12. All women who were working at the time of the first interview or who worked at all during 1966 or 1967 are considered to be working in the first year. Similarly, women who were employed at the 1977 interview or who worked any time since the 1976 interview are considered to be employed during the last year.

13. We are counting as training programs any job-related courses completed at regular educational institutions or vocational training schools, as well as company training provided by employers and correspondence courses. Because respondents were asked about "any training courses or educational programs of any kind, either on the job or elsewhere," we allow only that training which the respondent said she completed and used on her present job. In addition, if the program led to an additional year of formal education, that program was not counted as job training as well. Finally, participating in training programs varies widely among respondents in terms of intensity and job-relatedness. Further research on these issues is warranted by the fact that twice as many women as reported here partici-

pated in some kind of training program without regard to completion or job-relatedness.

14. Job training may include education or nursing courses that did not lead to an additional year of schooling completed.

15. The 1971 interview is excluded since weeks of unemployment are not available for the single year before the interview.

16. It should be remembered that these figures apply to women as they grow older. Looking at trends for one age group, women who were 40–44 in each year, unemployment in the later years is clearly higher than in the earlier years. The higher rates in early years shown in figure 1–9 were apparently due to the higher probability of unemployment when the group as a whole was younger.

17. These figures refer to women who are married and working at each point in time. Therefore, movement into and out of this group by persons of different characteristics could cause part of the observed changes.

18. The official poverty definition is based on the number of family members and whether the family lives on a farm. It is adjusted each year to reflect increases in the cost of living. The poverty levels for each family size and residence are published each year by the U.S. Bureau of the Census in the *Current Population Reports* (see, for example, U.S. Bureau of the Census 1979).

2

Problems of Labor-Market Reentry

Lois B. Shaw

What factors affect a woman's decision to reenter the labor market after a considerable absence? Do women who have spent many years outside the labor force have difficulty becoming reestablished? Is it harder for older women and for those who spend more time out? To what extent does a worsening economic climate create difficulties for reentrants?

These questions about labor-force reentry may be answered by studying women who return to employment after being out of the labor market for at least five years.[1] Here, reentry during the 1966–1971 period is compared with reentry during the 1971–1977 period to determine whether it became more difficult to enter the labor force as the economic climate worsened, the women grew older, and the average length of time away from the labor market increased. Precise estimates of the separate effects of recession, aging, and length of time out on reentry are difficult because these events happened simultaneously. On the other hand, the overlap of age groups in the two periods plus the facts that length of time away from employment differed greatly among individuals and economic conditions varied across the country make some estimation of separate effects possible.

Characteristics of Potential Reentrants

Information on the work activity of women in the NLS sample is available over an eleven-year period from 1966 to 1977. For comparison purposes, this span is separated into two periods, using the interview from the spring of 1971 as the dividing point.[2] In the first period, all women who had not worked since 1960 are considered to be potential reentrants; in the second, women who had not worked since 1965 are the potential reentrants.[3] The analysis is limited to white women who were married throughout the reentry period and the five preceding years. Although the reentry problems of black women and white women who lose a spouse are often urgent and their economic contributions may be crucial for family welfare, small sample sizes preclude analysis of their problems here.[4]

The author wishes to thank Theresa O'Brien and Alice Simon for their excellent research assistance.

33

Since the women studied here spent at least five years out of the labor force, they can be expected to differ from the entire sample, which includes women who spent shorter periods away from paid employment. Table 2–1 illustrates these differences by showing some characteristics of the two samples of potential reentrants compared with women who were already working or who had worked within the previous five years.

About 40 percent of white married women were potential reentrants in the first period, and their pattern of labor-market attachment was thus a common one among this generation of women. They had more and younger children at home than women who had current or recent work experience. Although the potential reentrants were only slightly younger than other women in the sample, they had about six fewer years of total work experience. On average, the income available to their families when they were not working was considerably greater than for families with working wives. Although as a group they were apparently more oriented to home activities and had less financial need to work, their educational attainment was simi-

Table 2–1
Characteristics of Potential Reentrants Compared with Women Who Were Working or Had Worked in the Previous Five Years

	1966–1971 Period		1971–1977 Period	
Characteristic	Potential Reentrants	Other Women	Potential Reentrants	Other Women
Percent				
Highest Grade Completed				
Less than high school	32	32	32	30
Some college	19	18	19	19
Family Composition				
With preschool children	52	34	32	15
With no children under 18	10	17	12	22
Mean				
Number of children at home	3.2	2.5	3.0	2.4
Prior work experience[a]	4.0	10.2	4.9	11.4
Years since last worked	13.9	—[b]	15.9	—[b]
Average other family income[c]	$19,100	$15,900	$22,500	$18,200
Age of respondent	36.1	36.4	40.8	41.2
Sample size	993	1,472	634	1,410

Note: All data refer to 1966 or 1967 for the first period and 1971 or 1972 for the second.
[a]Years worked six months or more since leaving school.
[b]Not shown because most women were currently employed.
[c]Family income without the wife's earnings, expressed in 1977 dollars.

lar to that of women who had returned to work earlier. The average woman in this group had been out of the labor force for fourteen years in 1966.[5]

Potential reentrants in the second period did not differ significantly in education from other women of their age, but they had postponed reentry beyond the average age chosen by most of their contemporaries. About a third still had preschool children, about the same proportion as the recently or currently working group five years previously. In this later time period, potential reentrants represented less than 30 percent of all married women.

Factors that Affect the Decision to Reenter the Labor Force

A woman's decision to reenter the labor force after a relatively long absence may be expected to depend on her family responsibilities, her health, the income available to the family if she does not work, the wage she might receive, and the difficulty of finding a suitable job. In addition, if she believes that women should not work when they have children or if she enjoys the activities involved in managing a home, she may be less likely to consider employment outside the home unless economic needs are pressing.[6]

These influences on reentry are included as explanatory variables in a logit analysis in which the dependent variable is labor-force reentry.[7] Family responsibilities are measured by the number and ages of children at the beginning of each period and whether a baby was born during the period. The difficulty of finding employment is measured by the average unemployment rate in the respondent's local labor market over the period of the interviews. Since actual wages prior to reentry are not available for these women, their earnings potential is represented by their educational level, their prior work experience, and the length of time since they last worked. The latter two variables probably also represent the respondent's preference for working outside the home in earlier years.

Most of these variables show only slightly different effects on the reentry decision in the two periods (table 2-2). Family composition is important in generally similar ways at both periods. The most common time to reenter was when the youngest child was moving beyond the primary grades or into high school. Women who had a new baby were much less likely to reenter. At the other end of the childbearing cycle, reentry after the empty-nest period had begun was less common than reentry at an earlier stage.

Supporting the view that reentry reflects economic pressures is the fact that the chances of reentry are greater the lower the family's income when the wife did not work. By the second period, there was a slight tendency for women with larger families to be more likely to reenter than those with small families. This tendency could be accounted for by greater financial

Table 2-2
Logit Analysis of Factors Related to Labor-Market Reentry
(numbers in parentheses are asymptotic t-ratios)

Independent Variables	1966–1971 Period		1971–1977 Period	
Youngest child age 0–5	.193	(1.32)	.226	(1.10)
Youngest child age 6–12	.311*	(2.09)	.434*	(2.43)
Youngest child age 13–17	.253	(1.34)	.306	(1.50)
Baby born[a]	−.243†	(−1.95)	−.475†	(−1.81)
Number of children at home	−.022	(−0.94)	.052†	(1.72)
Average other family income[a,b]	−.017**	(−4.35)	−.014**	(−3.49)
Highest grade completed	.056**	(3.45)	.038†	(1.89)
Prior work experience	.011	(1.09)	−.004	(−0.37)
Health problem (once)[a]	.225*	(2.03)	.065	(0.50)
Health problem (more than once)[a]	−.283**	(−2.62)	−.246*	(−1.99)
Moved[a]	.185†	(1.67)	.139	(1.04)
Role attitude	.072**	(4.87)	.047*	(2.32)
Liking for housework	.009	(0.13)	−.386**	(−4.36)
Average unemployment rate[a]	−.008	(−0.35)	−.016	(−0.64)
Years since last worked	−.008	(−1.00)	−.021*	(−2.34)
Constant	−1.254**	(−3.57)	−.600	(−1.39)
Log of likelihood function	−615.869		−377.904	
Mean of dependent variable	.393		.393	
Sample size	988		621	

Note: Variables are measured at the beginning of the reentry period with exceptions noted.
[a]During the reentry period.
[b]In thousands of 1977 constant dollars.
**Significant at the .01 level.
*Significant at the .05 level.
†Significant at the .10 level.

pressures as the children grew older and the cost of supplying their needs became greater.

In both periods a higher earnings potential was associated with reentry. However, this effect appears stronger in the first period than in the second as shown by the stronger influence of having more education in the earlier years. In the first period, reentry was not influenced by the amount of work experience prior to the absence from the labor force nor by the length of the absence itself. In the second period, however, the longer a woman had been out of the labor force, the less likely she was to return.[8] It may be that as the length of time since they had worked increased, this variable more closely reflected a preference for work at home.

Poor health that lasted long enough to be reported more than once inhibited reentry, but one report of poor health did not, and surprisingly in the first period, women who once reported a health problem were actually more likely to reenter than women who never reported one.

The average unemployment rate in the local market had no effect on reentry at either date. However, high unemployment can have two opposing effects: to discourage entry into the labor force or to encourage entry if the husband loses his job. Most previous research suggests that for white married women the discouragement effect is the stronger of the two.[9] In this case effects may be fairly evenly balanced. Also, variations in the unemployment rate over the period may mean that the average rate does not adequately reflect conditions at the time that reentry was being actively considered.

Attitudes toward women's roles were significantly at both periods. Women who believed that it is all right for women with children to work were more likely to be reentrants. Although attitudes toward housework did not affect reentry in the earlier period, by the later period women who enjoyed homemaking were much less likely to reenter employment than were women who expressed a lesser degree of enthusiasm for housework. Whether or not a woman enjoys work at home may become more important as family responsibilities lessen. When family responsibilities become less binding, homemaking versus market work may come to resemble an occupational choice, based not only on earnings potential but also on the relative satisfaction that a woman expects to receive from working outside the home as compared with the satisfaction of concentrating all her efforts on homemaking and child-care activities. The 1971–1977 results support the view that such an occupational choice has indeed been part of the reentry decision of middle-aged women in recent years.

Becoming Established in the Labor Force

By the end of the periods during which they had reentered, about one-third of the women had left the labor force. In order to determine why some women left and others did not, the two samples of reentrants are combined in a logit analysis of the factors affecting exit.[10] The same kinds of variables used to explain reentry are used to explain whether a woman continued to work after reentering. Age variables and length of the period away from work are included in order to determine whether women who are older or have been away from the labor market longer are less likely to remain in the labor force than younger women or those with more recent experience.

Effects of the economic climate on the likelihood of remaining in the labor force are represented by the unemployment rate in the local labor market and a period variable, which is added to capture any general differences in the economic environment of the two periods beyond those represented by area unemployment rates.

As table 2-3 shows, some of the variables most significant for reentry had little effect on whether a woman continued to work. Neither the family's income from other sources nor the number and ages of children

Table 2-3
Logit Analysis of Factors Related to Dropping Out of the Labor Force by the End of Reentry Period (Both Periods Combined)

	Logit Coefficient	Asymptotic t-Ratios
Highest grade completed	−.038†	(−1.88)
Prior work experience[a]	−.036**	(−2.71)
Youngest child age 0–5	−.019	(−0.09)
Youngest child age 6–12	−.185	(−1.10)
Youngest child age 13–17	−.140	(−0.87)
Number of children at home	.052	(1.57)
Other family income[b]	.004	(1.04)
Health problem	.276*	(2.10)
Moved[c]	.244	(1.13)
Role attitude[a]	−.010	(−0.49)
Liking for housework[a]	.148	(1.61)
Unemployment rate	.056**	(2.62)
Years since last worked[a]	−.011	(−1.12)
Entered before age 40	−.219†	(−1.90)
Entered age 45 or later	.151	(1.17)
Entered during 1971–1977 period	−.106	(−0.98)
Constant	.051	(0.11)
Log of likelihood function	−365.0	
Mean of dependent variable	.34	
Sample size	600	

Note: Variables are measured at the end of the reentry period with exceptions noted.
[a]At the beginning of the reentry period.
[b]In 1977 constant dollars.
[c]During the reentry period.
**Significant at the .01 level.
*Significant at the .05 level.
†Significant at the .10 level.

had an effect on leaving work after reentry. However, the more education and work experience the woman had before leaving the labor market, the more likely she was to continue at work once she had returned. The length of the absence had no effect, except that women who entered while they were in their thirties were much more likely to remain at work than older women. It may be that the market favors younger women and that women who enter at older ages are less likely to find good jobs.[11]

Women in areas with high unemployment rates were much more likely to leave than others. These newly hired workers probably faced a higher probability of layoff than more established workers. Whether they stopped working because of layoff or for other reasons, they might experience difficulty in finding other jobs if the local economy was not prosperous. Since unemployment rates were generally higher in the later period this meant that, other things equal, remaining employed was more difficult for the 1971-1977 reentrants. However, after taking the unemployment rate and other differences in the characteristics of the two groups into account, the reentrants in the relatively depressed later period were no more likely to drop out of the labor force than during the 1966-1971 period.

Wages of Reentrants

By definition, only those women who continue to work after reentry are becoming established in the labor market. However, among those who continue, the monetary rewards of work vary considerably. Women who continue to work, but at jobs that do not pay as well as their skills and experience should command, also show evidence of having difficulty in becoming established in the work force. Expressed in terms of 1977 dollars, the average wage of women who reentered in 1966-1971 was $3.54 per hour in 1971, while women who reentered in 1971-1977 had wages of only $3.18 in 1977. These lower wages of later reentrants did not merely reflect an overall decline of wages in the economy. During the same period, average hourly wages of all nonfarm private employees remained virtually constant in real terms at $5.16 in 1971 and $5.25 in 1977 (U.S. Department of Labor, 1979, p. 81).

Were the lower wages of the later reentrants due to being older, having experienced a longer absence from the labor market, or the worsening economic climate of the midseventies? This question may be answered by combining the two samples of reentrants and using the hourly wages of women who were working at the end of their respective reentry periods (1971 or 1977) as the dependent variable in a regression analysis.[12] Human-capital variables, labor-market variables, age, and a period-of-entry variable are the explanatory variables. As shown in table 2-4, more education led to

Table 2-4
Regression Equations for (ln) Wage Rate at End of Reentry Period

	Regression Coefficient	t-Ratio
Highest grade completed	.042**	(5.60)
Prior work experience[a]	.123	(1.29)
Weeks worked since reentry	.001**	(4.26)
Work week less than thirty-five hours	− .084*	(− 2.41)
Health problem	− .093†	(− 1.77)
Residence in the South	− .076†	(− 1.87)
Residence in an SMSA	.077*	(2.07)
Unemployment rate	− .003	(− 0.32)
Years since last worked[a]	.117	(0.58)
Entered before age 40	.019	(0.46)
Entered age 45 or later	.005	(0.11)
Entered during 1971–1977 period	− .082*	(− 2.18)
Constant	5.08	
$\bar{R}^2$	.18	
Mean of dependent variable	5.78	
Sample size	367	

[a]The exponential form $1 - e^{-x/10}$ is used to allow for a curvilinear relationship with the wage (see note 13).
**Significant at the .01 level.
*Significant at the .05 level.
†Significant at the .10 level.

higher wages, while working part time, having a health limitation, and living in the South led to lower wages. The amount of recent work experience had an important influence on wages, but experience acquired before leaving the labor force did not affect the wage after reentry.[13]

Two age variables represent reentry before age 40 and reentry at age 45 or later, with the omitted category ages 40–44. This method of measuring age effects is used to determine whether age discrimination may be affecting wages. It seems reasonable to expect that age discrimination would not increase in equal increments year by year, but rather increase abruptly at ages that are popularly felt to represent milestones. Measured this way, age had no independent effect on wages. Within the age range from the midthirties through midfifties, there is no evidence of age discrimination as far as the pay of recent labor-market entrants is concerned. Older women may experience more difficulty in finding good jobs and for this reason be less likely to enter or remain in the labor force, but those who do enter and remain appear to be as well paid as younger women.

Length of time out of the labor force did not significantly affect the wage.[14] This finding contrasts with that of past research by Mincer and Polachek (1974) and Mincer and Ofek (1982) who find large negative effects on wages as the period out of the labor force increases. They attribute this effect to decreases in marketable skills the longer a woman remains out of the labor market. The results of the present analysis suggest that any such effect must operate in the first five years of absence.[15] Beyond this period the length of time out appears to make no difference to the wages of entrants. For midlife women, it is encouraging to find that long absences from the labor force are not penalized more than short ones. For younger women, who are spending much shorter periods away from employment than middle-aged women did (Mott and Shapiro 1978), it will be discouraging if short absences are those most penalized. However, more research is needed on reentry after short periods. In particular, the economic climate when reentry occurs should be taken into account, as well as the possibly confounding effects of age at reentry.

The negative coefficient on the time-period variable indicates that, after controlling for other relevant characteristics, the 1977 wages of women who reentered in the second period were 8 percent below the 1971 wages of first-period reentrants. This difference could be attributed to the worsening economic climate of the mid-1970s. However, the unemployment rate in the local labor market had no effect on the wage rate.[16] Another possible explanation of these lower wages is that women who enter the labor force after a long absence may be competing for jobs with young women who also have little work experience.[17] Women who reentered in the late sixties shared a job market with young women born before or during World War II. The larger number of children born in the postwar period was only beginning to reach the labor market by 1971, but by the midseventies, almost all of the baby-boom children were of working age. Further, because of late marriage and low fertility, their labor-force participation was higher than that of previous generations. Therefore, competition for jobs that did not require much experience probably increased significantly. A slower rate of economic growth would compound the difficulty of finding good jobs for both young and middle-aged women.

Summary and Conclusions

Women's reentry into the labor force after a relatively long absence was investigated in order to determine whether the length of time away, the age of the woman, and the economic climate in the period from 1966 to 1977 affected who reentered and the ease or difficulty of becoming established in the work force. Although it is difficult to distinguish the separate effects of these conditions because the women were growing older, the length of time they were out of the labor market was increasing, and economic conditions were worsening at approximately the same time, each has been taken into account to the extent possible.

Women in our sample were a little more likely to reenter the labor force while they were in their thirties than in their forties or fifties. As they reached their forties, those women who had been away longest were least likely to reenter, but women who had not expressed strong enthusiasm for homemaking often returned to work at this time. There was no evidence that high rates of unemployment discouraged reentry for these women. However, a third of the reentrants did not remain in the labor market until the end of the five or six year period during which they had reentered. Women living in high unemployment areas were much more likely to leave the labor force than were women in other places. Women who had reentered while in their forties or fifties were more likely to leave than younger women.

The wages received by the women who did remain in the labor force were strongly related to their education and recent work experience. However, the length of time they had been away from paid employment had no effect on their wages. Thus, since all of the women had been out of the labor force for at least five years, if absence from the labor force does have an adverse effect of market skills, it must be felt in the first years of absence.

Older women did not have lower wages than younger women. Any age discrimination within the age range from the midthirties to midfifties must operate either beyond entry-level jobs or in hiring decisions that make it difficult for older women to obtain employment. Their higher drop-out rate suggests that older women may have difficulty in finding or keeping good jobs. Most striking was the general deterioration in the wages of reentering women between 1971 and 1977. These lower wages may have been due to increasing competition for entry-level jobs between older women and the large baby-boom cohort that was in its twenties by 1977. A period of more rapid economic growth would erase the labor-market entry problems of both groups.

Notes

1. Only women who actually become employed for at least two weeks are considered reentrants here. About 3 percent of potential reentrants reported looking for work but never became employed. Considering only

the employed women in the analysis of labor-force entry follows the usage of Heckman (1979).

2. This division was chosen because in the latter period, information on work activity is available for only four of the six years; the year before the interviews in the spring of 1972, 1974, 1976, and 1977. Starting the second period with the year between the 1971 and 1972 interviews gives us data for the beginning and ending year of this period, while having a 1972 cutoff date would start the second period with a year for which information is missing. Throughout, I assume that work activity during the four years for which data are available is typical of the entire six years.

3. Information on whether a woman had worked during the 1961-1965 period came from the question asked in 1967, "When did you last work at a job lasting two consecutive weeks or more?" Women who worked only one week from time to time during 1961-1965 may be included as potential entrants during 1966-1971. To be considered a potential reentrant in 1971-1977 a woman could not be employed for more than one week in any of the 1966-1971 interview years.

4. Over 80 percent of these women had worked at some time during the five-year periods before the reentry years examined here and, therefore, are not eligible to be considered potential reentrants. The problems that follow marital dissolution are examined in chapter 7.

5. Women who had never worked were counted as potential reentrants, although the term *entrant* rather than *reentrant* would be more appropriate for them. In 1966 about 10 percent of potential reentrants had never worked. For purposes of calculating years since last worked, they were assigned age 16 as the time of their last job.

6. This analysis follows the theory of female labor supply as developed by Mincer (1962), Cain (1966), Bowen and Finegan (1969), and others. Important effects of sex-role attitudes on work decisions have been shown by Waite (1979), Macke et al. (1978), and Shaw (1980).

7. Specifically, the dependent variable is a dummy with a value of one if a woman is employed for more than one week in any year during the period and a value of zero otherwise. The requirement of at least two weeks of employment in a year in order to be considered a reentrant is made for consistency with the definition of years not working (see note 3).

8. When age was entered as a variable in the analysis, younger women in the first period were found to be significantly more likely to reenter than older women. In the second, length of time out of the work force remained significant, but age was not.

9. See Blau (1978). However, Wachter (1972) found a positive effect of unemployment for older workers.

10. The dependent variable is dichotomous, taking the value of one if a reentrant was not in the labor force at the last interview in her reentry period, and zero otherwise.

11. Age could also represent a long-term preference for nonmarket activities not captured in the homemaking variable. Age does not represent the effect of length of time out of the labor force prior to reentry since the latter is not significant even when the age variables are omitted from the analysis.

12. The natural logarithm of the hourly wage (in cents per hour) is used since coefficients on independent variables then express effects in percentage terms rather than in absolute amounts. When comparing a wide wage range, percentage changes are more meaningful than changes expressed in cents per hour.

13. For both years of work experience and years out of the labor force, I use the functional form $1 - e^{-x/10}$ where x = years. The desirable property of this form is that the effect of each additional year is smaller as experience (time out) increases (Griliches 1976). The variables take values from 0 to about .95 as years increase from 0 to 30.

14. This result is not sensitive to the exact specification of the model. Years since last worked was significant neither in linear form nor when the age and period variables were omitted from the equation. When the sample was limited to women who were age 40–48 at the end of their reentry period, the coefficient on years since worked became negative but not significant. (The t-ratio was $-.8$.)

15. The longest absence in Mincer and Ofek is seven years. See also Daymont and Statham, chapter 4, this book. However, Sandell and Shapiro (1978) and Corcoran (1979b) find much smaller effects of absence from the labor force on wages than do Mincer and his colleagues. Strober (1979) contests the view that lower wages of reentrants (if they exist) are necessarily due to skill loss. Lack of seniority and policies against training older workers for higher level positions might lead to lower wages regardless of the worker's basic skills.

16. The unemployment rate was not significant even when the period variable was excluded from the equation.

17. That young people of both sexes are substitutes for older women in the labor market is suggested by recent research by Grant and Hammermesh (1980).

3 Causes of Irregular Employment Patterns

Lois B. Shaw

Why do some women become established as continuous workers while others work irregularly? Do women leave employment largely for such personal reasons as extensive family duties, poor health, high income, or increasing income adequacy as children leave home, or are the important causes related to the state of the job market? In 1975–1976 was the recession an important factor? Are women with the least education and work experience most likely to have difficulty in remaining steadily employed as the economic climate worsens?

Although most of the married women in the NLS sample had some work experience outside the home between 1966 and 1977, only 30 percent of white and 45 percent of black women worked as much as 75 percent of the weeks during these years.[1] Intermittent work and reentry after an absence from the work force were common, and some women left the labor force entirely. Chapter 1 showed that women who worked irregularly did not make the wage and occupational gains enjoyed by continuously employed workers. This chapter looks at the reasons for the irregular employment patterns that were so costly to progress in the working world. Whereas chapter 2 focused on reentry, this one focuses on women who left the work force for short or long periods between 1971 and 1977.

Description of Work Patterns

Information on women's work activity is available over the eleven-year period 1966–1977. In order to describe the varied patterns of work activity that women experience, these eleven years are divided into the two segments described in chapter 2, 1966–1971 and 1971–1977, with the interview in the spring of 1971 as the dividing point.[2] Within each segement, three work-attachment categories are defined: no work outside the home lies at one end of the scale, strong attachment at the other, and intermediate attachment between these extremes. Those who worked at least six months in each year

Theresa O'Brien, Alice Simon, and Woo Cho provided expert research assistance for this chapter.

45

of a period are defined as *strongly* (or continuously) *attached*. Those who worked for less than six months in any year but at least two weeks in at least one year are defined as having an *intermediate attachment*.[3] This latter group consists of women with a history of intermittent employment as well as women who were entering or leaving the labor force during the given period. Although these definitions are necessarily arbitrary, their purpose is to include in the intermediate category workers who experience interruptions of paid employment that are sufficiently long to be a potential source of hardship.[4]

Patterns of women's employment over the eleven years can be characterized by their movements between work-attachment categories in the two consecutive periods. During the 1971–1977 period, about one-quarter of both white and black women who had been working continuously during the previous five years had an interruption of employment lasting at least six months, while the other three-quarters remained strongly attached. About 35 percent of the women who were initially in the intermediate attachment category became strongly attached in 1971–1977 while about one-half remained in the intermediate category and 15 percent dropped out of the labor force entirely.

Factors that Affect Work Patterns

What determines whether women continue to work and whether they work steadily or intermittently? In answering these questions, the major emphasis will be on two central issues. First, is there evidence that economic conditions prevented women from working when they would have preferred to do so? Second, are there differences between women with strong and intermediate attachments both in their vulnerability to economic conditions, as might be expected, as well as in other factors that lead to work interruptions? Leaving the labor force after at least five years of employment is probably a qualitative different decision from leaving only a few weeks after reentry. In the former case, not only are the foregone earnings likely to be greater, but a long-standing life style is changed. In the latter, little has been invested in the job, and the woman returns to the familiar life style of work in the home.[5]

Women with an intermediate attachment in 1966–1971 could leave the work force, increase their attachment (become strongly attached), or remain in the intermediate category during the next six years.[6] Since there are three possibilities, multinomial logit is used to examine the determinants of changes in their work attachment. Women who were strongly attached rarely left employment completely; therefore, only the alternatives of continuing to work steadily or decreasing to an intermediate level of attachment are examined for this group. The explanatory variables in these analyses include personal and family conditions: family composition, health problems, income without the wife's earnings, and whether the family moved. Also included are education, previous work experience, and the area unemployment rate, which influence the wage a women can command and whether she can find a satisfactory job.[7]

Women with Intermediate Attachment in 1966-1971

For women who were not previously well established in the labor market, determinants of leaving the labor market and of becoming strongly attached are shown in table 3-1. In each case the comparison group consists of women who remained in the intermediate category in 1971-1977.[8] White women who had preschool children in 1971 were more likely to leave the work force for the entire period than were women whose children already had reached elementary school by 1971 and junior or senior high school by 1977. At the opposite end of the childrearing cycle, white women whose children were already grown in 1971 were about as likely to leave as were mothers of young children. White women who were past the childrearing years were also least likely to increase their work attachment. Strong attachment was most likely to begin when children were moving beyond elementary school, while they were in high school, or immediately after the high school years. However, the ages of their children had only weak effects on the work attachment of black women.

High income from husband's earnings or other sources led white women to leave the labor force entirely or maintain an intermediate level of attachment. For black women, increases in income caused dropping out or intermediate attachment, although continuously high income had no effect on the degree of attachment. Health was a factor in long-term exits for black women but not for white. Health problems kept women of both races from increasing their attachment. Moving from one city or county to another prevented white women but not black from becoming strongly attached. Since black women's share of family earnings tends to be higher than that of white wives, it may be the case that black families are more likely to consider both spouse's job prospects before moving (Sandell 1976).

Earnings potential, as represented by education and work experience in the previous five years, was important in determining which women would become strongly attached, especially among white women. For white women, but not for black, education strongly influenced the chances of increasing attachment. However, education made little difference between intermediate attachment and exit. For both races, recent work experience was a good predictor of whether a woman would become strongly attached,

Table 3-1
Multinomial Logit Equations: Determinants of Work Attachment in 1971-1977 for Women with Intermediate Attachment in 1966-1971
(asymtotic t-ratios in parentheses)

	Whites		Blacks	
	No Work	Strong Attachment	No Work	Strong Attachment
Age of youngest child				
0-5	−.001	.307	−.813	−.202
	(−0.00)	(0.83)	(−0.94)	(−0.29)
6-12	−.718*	.596†	−.971	−.145
	(−2.00)	(1.94)	(−1.20)	(−0.23)
13-17	−.435	.701*	−.527	−.154
	(−1.26)	(2.31)	(−0.64)	(−0.23)
Baby born	−.570	−1.711**	−.021	.836
	(−0.83)	(−2.59)	(−0.02)	(1.04)
Number of children	−.132	.040	−.133	−.099
	(−1.52)	(0.61)	(−1.15)	(−1.05)
Other family income	.027*	−.033**	−.076	.012
	(2.01)	(−2.72)	(−1.29)	(0.28)
Change in average income	.020	.033*	.169*	−.086
	(1.13)	(2.22)	(2.03)	(−1.64)
Health problem	.089	−.348**	.298†	−.375*
	(1.08)	(−4.13)	(1.86)	(−2.35)
Moved	−.022	−.993**	−1.49	−.215
	(−0.08)	(−3.75)	(−1.20)	(−0.23)
Highest grade completed	−.058	.174**	−.050	−.128†
	(−1.17)	(4.38)	(−0.59)	(−1.68)
Prior work experience	.039*	.013	−.023	.008
	(2.13)	(0.83)	(−0.81)	(0.36)
Percent of weeks worked	−.029**	.021**	−.032**	.045**
	(−5.82)	(6.33)	(−3.09)	(5.35)
Average unemployment rate	.089	−.000	.243*	.021
	(1.43)	(−0.00)	(2.41)	(0.24)
Constant	−.453	−3.11**	−.000	−.830
	(−0.64)	(−5.16)	(−0.00)	(−0.68)
Sample size	897	897	234	234
Log likelihood function	−773.46	−773.46	−177.01	−177.01
Mean choice probabilities[a]	.15	.35	.17	.35

[a]Choice probabilities sum to 1. The omitted category, intermediate attachment, has a choice probability of .50 for whites and .48 for blacks.
**Significant at the .01 level.
*Significant at the .05 level.
†Significant at the .10 level.

remain in intermediate attachment, or leave the labor market. Earlier work experience, in contrast, was generally not important.[9]

The relatively high unemployment rates of this period increased the amount of long-term leaving by black women. For white women the effect of unemployment rates was smaller, only bordering on statistical significance. On the other hand, high unemployment did not affect the chances of becoming strongly attached for either race.[10] The absence of such an effect could reflect either the fact that women do not generally leave the labor force in times of high unemployment or the fact that the average unemployment rate in the area varies over the period; however, replacing the average unemployment rate with the rate in 1976, a year of high overall unemployment, did not change these results.

Women with Strong Attachment, 1966-1971

In contrast to the situation for less-established workers, no significant effects of family composition are observed in the work patterns of women who were already strongly attached and had worked fairly continuously in the 1966-1971 period (table 3-2). Although few of these women had young children, a large majority had children at home, at least at the beginning of the 1971-1977 period. Even with children present, once the women had a history of continuous work, family considerations that are measured here did not cause them to work less. In fact, the larger their families the more likely black women were to work continuously, probably due to financial pressures.

The amount of income available if they did not work likewise had no effect on the work activity of the well-established married women workers. For white women, this lack of income effect contrasts sharply with the effects of income on becoming strongly attached, on long-term leaving, and on reentering after a long absence (see chapter 2).[11] Once a family becomes accustomed to a wife's earnings, two incomes are probably built into their long-term plans regardless of the level of the husband's earnings. However, an increase in income other than the woman's earnings did have a barely significant negative effect on the amount she worked.

We must look to factors besides family composition or income to explain decreasing versus continuing attachment. Health problems were an important cause of working less, especially for black women. For white women moving also had this effect. For both races, the better-educated women were most likely to continue working steadily, and the more previous work experience a woman had (and for these women early experience was important) the more likely she was to remain strongly attached. All of these factors point to the importance of high-earnings

Table 3-2
Logit Equations: Determinants of Intermediate Attachment in 1971-1977
for Women with Strong Attachment in 1966-1971
(asymtotic t-ratios in parentheses)

	Whites	*Blacks*
Age of youngest child		
0-5	.040	.056
	(0.13)	(0.11)
6-12	-.204	.099
	(-1.01)	(0.28)
13-17	-.208	-.105
	(-1.18)	(-0.32)
Baby born	.172	.285
	(0.38)	(0.43)
Number of children	-.066	-.149†
	(-1.12)	(-1.65)
Other family income	-.006	.013
	(-0.66)	(0.52)
Change in average income	.019†	-.010
	(1.75)	(-0.35)
Health problem	.110*	.349**
	(1.97)	(3.55)
Moved	.546**	a
	(2.61)	
Highest grade completed	-.112**	-.092*
	(-4.22)	(-2.44)
Prior work experience	-.021*	-.024
	(-2.12)	(-1.18)
Percent of weeks worked	-.036**	-.018
	(-4.01)	(-0.99)
Average unemployment rate	-.007	.040
	(-0.20)	(0.61)
Constant	4.648**	2.046
	(4.88)	(1.15)
Sample size	453	153
Log likelihood function	-225.905	-71.220
Mean of dependent variable	.26	.25

[a]Not included in model due to small number of movers.
**Significant at the .01 level.
*Significant at the .05 level.
†Significant at the .10 level.

potential as an incentive for continuous work for this group. High levels of past work experience also could indicate strong preferences for working outside the home. High unemployment rates did not appear to cause problems of work loss for these women. However, the decrease in attachment of women with less education and experience could indicate some difficulty in remaining continuously employed regardless of the unemployment rate in the area in which they lived.

Examples of Work Patterns

To show the magnitude of some of the most important effects just discussed, table 3-3 illustrates work attachment probabilities during 1971–1977 for women with various characteristics.[12] For white women, income influences the subsequent work activity of those without a strong attachment but does not influence women who are strongly attached. The effects of moving to another area are large: the probability of increasing attachment from intermediate to strong is cut in half while the probability of decreasing attachment from strong to intermediate doubles in white high-income families that move. College graduates have a very high probability of becoming or remaining strongly attached. They are nearly twice as likely to become strongly attached as women who only completed ninth grade, and their chances of remaining strongly attached are nearly 40 percent higher.

Although the logit analysis did not reveal any significant effects of family composition on the strongly attached group, here we see that the effect of having fewer children as the older ones leave home is similar to the effect noted earlier for women in the intermediate category. At the stage when their children are grown and financial pressures lessen, women are less likely to become strongly attached to the labor force and more likely to leave or to decrease their attachment than women at earlier stages of child-rearing. Some women who went to work to help children attend college may drop out when their children's education is complete. However, it is still only a minority that work less or leave entirely.

For black women the effects of family composition and family income are rather small and uneven and, therefore, are not shown. The most dramatic effects are those caused by poor health. Having a health problem at two interviews doubles the chances of long-term leaving and almost triples the chances of moving from strong to intermediate attachment for black women with grown children. In addition, the chances of becoming strongly attached are reduced greatly. While white women who reported health problems twice had about the same probabilities of being in each work category as their black counterparts, the reductions in work attach-

Table 3-3
Work-Attachment Probabilities during 1971–1977 by 1966–1971 Attachment for Married Women with Specified Family and Personal Characteristics

Age of Youngest Child in 1971	Number of Children	Other Characteristics[a]	Intermediate 1966–1971			Strong 1966–1971	
			No Work[b]	Intermediate[b]	Strong[b]	Intermediate[b]	Strong[b]
Whites							
0–5	3	Income = $11,000	.10	.44	.46	.30	.70
0–5	3	Income = $25,000	.16	.51	.33	.27	.73
0–5	3	Income = $25,000, moved	.20	.65	.16	.53	.47
6–12	2	Highest grade completed = 9	.10	.56	.35	.35	.65
6–12	2	Highest grade completed = 16	.04	.31	.66	.10	.90
0–5	3	———	.12	.48	.40	.28	.72
6–12	2	———	.07	.45	.48	.22	.78
13–17	2	———	.08	.42	.50	.22	.78
18 or over	1	———	.18	.53	.30	.32	.68
18 or over	1	Health problem twice	.24	.60	.17	.43	.57
Blacks							
18 or over	1	No health problem	.13	.46	.41	.18	.82
18 or over	1	Health problem twice	.25	.50	.24	.46	.54

Note: Calculated from logit equations in tables 3–1 and 3–2.

[a] Values for other characteristics are set at the means of the explanatory variables for the two 1966–1971 attachment groups unless otherwise specified. In the case of noncontinuous variables, the modal category is used.

[b] Work attachment for 1971–1977.

ment caused by poor health were not as large. Poor health is an important component of the economic problem experienced by some middle-aged women, and black women are especially vulnerable, as chapter 6 will demonstrate in greater detail.

Reasons for Leaving Employment as Reported by the
Women Themselves

Although much of the intermittent work of middle-aged women appears to be due to health problems, family constraints, or preferences for remaining at home if their husband's earnings permit, economic conditions and low skill levels also may have limited the work opportunities of some women. To explore further the causes of irregular work patterns, we examine the reasons given by both job changers and leavers for leaving their most recent job. Table 3–4 shows the percentage of women who list business conditions, other working conditions, family reasons, health and other not-readily classifiable reasons for leaving their most recent jobs: reasons are shown for major work-attachment categories. Women without major work interruptions, both those becoming strongly attached and those working continuously for the eleven years, are shown for purposes of comparison. (Many of the latter reported no job change. Reasons shown are for those who did change employers.)

Business conditions—including the end of temporary or seasonal jobs as well as layoffs, slack work, and plant closings—accounted for 25 to 30 percent of the job leaving for black women whose attachment became or remained intermediate and for all white women except the most strongly attached. Some of this job leaving may have been voluntary in the sense that the job was originally undertaken because it was temporary and fit into family plans. However, nearly half of the women citing business conditions as the reason for leaving experienced some unemployment, and a quarter of white women and a third of black were unemployed for three months or more. These figures suggest that considerable involuntary job leaving was not well captured by the area unemployment rate variables in the logit analyses.

The women's own reasons for leaving also show that family reasons were more important for some groups than suggested by logit analyses in which family responsibilities can only be approximated by looking at numbers and ages of children. Although logit analysis showed little evidence that children affect the work activity of black women, about one-fourth of black women who remained in the intermediate category gave family reasons for job leaving. Thirty percent of white long-term leavers also cited family reasons for leaving, although in the logit analysis the probability of long-term exit was increased only moderately by the presence of

Table 3–4
Reason Given for Leaving Most Recent Job, by Work-Attachment Categories
(percentage distributions)

Reason Given	Intermediate Attachment 1966–1971			Strong Attachment 1966–1971	
	No Work[a]	Intermediate[a]	Strong[a]	Intermediate[a]	Strong[a]
Whites					
Business conditions	25	32	29	29	15
Working conditions	11	15	25	19	33
Family	30	23	18	19	13
Health	16	13	3	19	8
Other	17	17	25	14	32
Total percent	100	100	100	100	100
Sample size	107	412	133	96	82
Blacks					
Business conditions	19	27	14	29	5
Working conditions	11	16	21	4	25
Family	15	24	6	18	15
Health	40	20	17	30	7
Other	15	13	42	20	48
Total percent	100	100	100	100	100
Sample size	31	109	39	31	32

[a]Work attachment in 1971–1977.

young children.[13] Family circumstances, such as children or other family members with illnesses or other special needs that require extra care, or simply the difficulty of keeping up with both housework and work outside the home when children are present, may cause a woman to leave a job regardless of how old her chilren are or how many are present.

The finding that poor health is one of the most important reasons for intermittent work and long-term exits among black women is confirmed by the women's stated reasons for leaving their jobs. Fully 40 percent of women who left the work force for the entire 1971–1977 period gave health as their reason for leaving. Health was the most important single reason given for decreases from strong to intermediate attachment as well.

Intermittent Work and Unemployment

In order to look further at possible involuntary components of irregular work patterns, we show in table 3–5 the percentage of women experiencing

Table 3-5
Weeks Unemployed 1971-1977, by Work-Attachment Categories
(percentage distributions)

Weeks Unemployed	Intermediate Attachment 1966-1971			Strong Attachment 1966-1971	
	No Work[a]	Intermediate[a]	Strong[a]	Intermediate[a]	Strong[a]
Whites					
None	92	68	85	59	90
1-13	7	17	8	14	7
14 or more	1	14	7	27	3
Total percent	100	100	100	100	100
Sample size	146	476	324	124	353
Blacks					
None	93	56	80	66	85
1-13	5	16	14	14	6
14 or more	2	28	5	20	9
Total percent	100	100	100	100	100
Sample size	45	122	86	39	118

[a]Work attachment in 1971-1977.

unemployment over the six years.[14] Two groups of women experienced considerable unemployment: those who remained in the intermediate category, and those whose attachment decreased from strong to intermediate. Between 30 and 45 percent of women in these groups were unemployed at some time during the six years, and the percentage with more than three months (thirteen weeks) of unemployment ranged from 15 to nearly 30 percent. More unemployment could be expected for these groups than for their steadily employed counterparts since intermittent work may require job search when reentering the labor force. Nevertheless, the amount of unemployment experienced suggests that some women had difficulty in finding jobs.

In the logit analysis, high area unemployment rates were associated with long-term leaving. However, women who were long-term leavers experienced very little unemployment. The reason for this discrepancy is not clear. It is possible that some of these women lived in areas of chronically high unemployment, and if they lost a job, were discouraged from looking for work by the poor prospects of finding another one. In fact, at the time of the 1977 interview about one-fifth or white and one-sixth of black long-term leavers said they would probably or definitely accept a job if one were offered to them. While these responses may be an overestimate of actual desire for work, they probably represent considerable numbers of discouraged work seekers as well.

That the 1971–1977 period was kinder to the employment prospects of strongly attached workers than to those who were not so well established can be seen from the 1977 circumstances of the two groups. About 85 percent of the entire group with a strong attachment during the 1966–1971 period were employed in 1977; about 7 percent were looking for work or had a continuing interest in employment; and 8 percent were out of the labor force and no longer interested in employment. In contrast, of the original intermediate group, 56 percent were employed in 1977; 14 percent were unemployed or willing to accept a job; and the remaining 30 percent were not interested in employment. Although a small group of women with a previous record of continuous work had unemployment problems in the 1971–1977 period, unemployment and perhaps some discouragement due to the state of the labor market are concentrated in the larger group of less experienced workers.

Summary and Conclusions

The reasons for noncontinuous employment vary among middle-aged married women. Our major purpose has been to determine the extent to which such work patterns are responses to family and personal constraints and preferences and to what extent they reflect poor job opportunities for middle-aged women in recent years.[15] Of course, preferences and opportunities interact. Working in the home may be preferred to accepting a poorly paid or monotonous job, whereas a more interesting or better paid job would be preferred to being a full-time homemaker. A woman may want to work only part-time but not be able to find a part-time job. The purpose here was not to make precise judgments about the relative importance of personal and labor-market influences but rather to identify cases in which women's intermittent work was due to personal constraints or preferences and others in which women wanted to work but became unemployed or discouraged about finding employment.

Family responsibilities remained an important reason for irregular work patterns for women in their mid-thirties to mid-fifties. Health was an important cause of intermittent employment and long periods out of the work force, especially among black women. High family income allowed some women to work intermittently or to leave the labor force entirely. However, women who had worked steadily for at least five years were not likely to decrease their attachment in response to high family income. A family's migration to another area often resulted in interruption of employment for white women. All of these reasons for irregular work patterns suggest family or health constraints or personal preferences that were not strongly influenced by the state of the job market.

On the other hand, high unemployment rates in some areas affected the work behavior of women who had not previously become well established in the labor market. Unemploment and job leaving for business reasons were also common among women who had not worked steadily in the preceding five years. Among women who had worked most of the time in the recent past, a small minority, generally the less educated, also experienced job loss due to business conditions and considerable unemployment. Chapter 2 found that women who were new labor-market reentrants left the labor force again in areas of high unemployment, and wages of reentrants were found to have worsened in recent years. All of these circumstances point to labor-market problems for middle-aged women who have little recent work experience or low levels of education.

Middle-aged married women are often thought of as secondary workers, yet many of them will need to work in the future if they become widowed or divorced or their family income becomes inadequate. For such women, time spent out of the labor force involuntary may make self-support or contributing to family income increasingly difficult in the future.

Notes

1. Only women who were married throughout the 1966–1977 period are considered in this chapter. Women whose marriages ended are the subject of chapter 7. The number of never-married women is too small for separate analysis.

2. As mentioned in chapter 2, there are two years of missing data in the 1971–1977 period: 1972–1973 and 1974–1975. In each case the missing period is from the interview in the spring of one year until the next spring. It is assumed here that the four years of available data are representative of the entire six years. This assumption may cause the amount of intermittent work to be slightly underestimated.

3. Women who never worked for more than one week in a year are included in the *no-work* category. Generally no information is available on casual one-week jobs. This definition is congruent with the reentry definition in chapter 2. Neither decreasing the lower boundary of the intermediate category to one week nor increasing it to eight changed the results of the analysis substantially.

4. It does not seem appropriate to include in the intermediate category the many women who regularly work less than a full year because they are employed by school systems as teachers, service workers, or clerical staff. These women are essentially continuous workers. Similarly, I did not want to include women who experienced short-term layoffs from regular jobs or who lost a few weeks of work when they changed jobs. However, for pur-

poses of identifying possible labor-market problems, it is important not to exclude women who have difficulty in finding and keeping a steady job.

5. Although labor-supply theory originally treated these decisions as equivalent, in recent years increasing attention has been paid to the effects of past work history on current employment. State dependence, when past work experience directly influences the probability of present employment, may be due to the higher earnings potential that work experience brings or to fixed costs of labor-market entry that make continuous spells of employment likely (Heckman 1979; Cogan 1979). Differences in the amount of work experience in the past may also reflect unobserved differences in tastes, abilities, or home or labor market constraints (Heckman 1979; Heckman and Willis 1977). Studies of labor-force entry and exit have found differences in the factors that affect work decisions starting from these two states (Long and Jones 1980; Blau 1978).

6. Those who did no work at all during the 1971–1977 period had left employment before the period began. For convenience they will be referred to as *leavers*.

7. Most of these variables have been widely used in the analysis of labor-force participation from such early research as Cain (1966) and Bowen and Finegan (1969) in economics, and Sweet (1973) in sociology to the present (Heckman 1979; Stephan and Schroeder 1979; Long and Jones 1980). The effect of interarea migration on married women's work has been studied by Sandell (1976). Women who were strongly attached in 1966–1971 differed considerably from those in the intermediate group along these dimensions. Women who were strongly attached in this earlier period were older, with fewer family responsibilities and more prior work experience than women with intermediate attachment. Among white women, income available from sources other than their own earnings was higher in the intermediate group than in the strongly attached group, while among black women the reverse was true. Among white women, little difference appeared between the two groups in average education, but strongly attached black women had considerably more education than those in the intermediate category.

8. In multinomial logit with three choices there are two dichotomous dependent variables. In the present case one dependent variable takes a value of one for leavers and zero for remaining in the intermediate category; the other takes a value of one for strong attachment and zero for remaining in the intermediate category. The coefficients on the explanatory variables are constrained so that the probabilities of being in each category will sum to one. See Schmidt and Strauss (1975) for a more complete description of multinomial logit analysis.

9. The more work experience white women had before 1966 the more likely they were to leave the labor force. This may reflect in part an age effect.

10. At first, these results may appear to be different from those of past research, which finds high unemployment rates discouraging labor-market entry but not encouraging exit (see, for example, Blau 1978). However, the long-run leavers were a group who did not reenter over the 1971–1977 period and may have been deterred by high unemployment. The finding that high unemployment rates did not deter strong attachment agrees with past research that shows that exits are not affected by high unemployment. One anomaly should be noted, however. The biggest effects of unemployment on long-run leavers were found for black women, who have in the past been thought to have an increased probability of entering the labor force when unemployment was high.

11. Similar results have been reported by Long and Jones (1980), who found that family income affects the labor-force entry but not exit between two dates, and by Stephan and Schroeder (1979) who found that family income did not affect the work activity of women who had already demonstrated a strong work commitment.

12. The probabilities are calculated from the logit equations shown in tables 3–1 and 3–2.

13. Family reasons included moving as well as reasons concerning children or other family members. However, moving also showed no effect for black women or white long-term leavers.

14. The figures shown are conservative estimates of the amount of unemployment, since in cases where no information was available it was assumed that no unemployment had occurred. According to Morgenstern and Barrett (1974), retrospective information on weeks of unemployment also understates the true amount for women below age 45.

15. The term *preferences* as used in economics often disguises constraints. For example, as chapter 5 shows, women are influenced by their perceptions of their husbands' attitudes toward their working. Some women who would like to work may feel that their husbands are opposed. Such women may prefer not to work rather than cause strain in their marriages. Similarly the opinion of friends and neighbors may constrain choices.

4 Occupational Atypicality: Changes, Causes, and Consequences

Thomas Daymont and
Anne Statham

The changes in women's work experience depend not only on their patterns of labor-force participation but also on the type of work they do. Women of all ages have typically been segregated into clerical, retail sales and service occupations, and private household work, all of which bring lower-than-average job rewards (Oppenheimer 1970). Earnings in these occupations are much lower than in male-dominated occupations, even after controlling for education and skill requirements (McLaughlin 1978; Jusenius 1976). Further, the occupations in which women are concentrated also tend to allow little job authority and few other important rewards. Although many women attain professional status as teachers, nurses, and social workers, even these professions entail little supervision over other workers or control over resources, and they provide limited chances for advancement. To the extent this segregation continues, then, women's opportunities to participate fully at all levels of society will be quite limited, despite their increasing labor-force participation.

This chapter examines several important questions about occupational segregation. Has there been any decrease in women's tendency to be in female (or typical) occupations during the 1967 to 1977 period, a time of apparently intense change in attitudes about women's roles? Have any potential improvements in women's situations been eliminated by the stagnant economic conditions of the 1970s? What are the determinants of occupational atypicality? Are women disproportionately in typical or female occupations because of family constraints and weak labor-market commitment, as some have argued? If so, attempts to reduce segregation might profitably concentrate on alleviating the family constraints on women and improving their human capital accumulation. What are the consequences of being in a typically female occupation? Does it affect earnings? Has this effect changed over time?

The authors wish to acknowledge the research assistance of Don Larrick in the preparation of this chapter.

Conceptual Issues: Social Forces Affecting Atypicality

Change in Occupational Atypicality

Following the definition of occupational atypicality constructed by Jusenius (1976), if women comprise a smaller proportion of an occupation than they comprise of the entire labor force (approximately 33 percent), then that occupation is considered to be atypical. Previous research suggests that there has been little if any increase in women's tendency to enter atypical (or male typed) occupations in recent years (U.S. Commission on Civil Rights 1978; Blau and Hendricks 1979; Beller 1980; England 1980). Even less change toward atypicality could be expected among this particular sample of women, for several reasons. First, our sample does not include younger women, and what little change has been found in previous studies may be due largely to younger women's having chosen less traditional occupations as they moved into the labor force. Mature women are likely to have already developed specific occupational skills that may help create an occupational inertia.

Although little change overall may appear among the women in our sample, significant amounts of change may exist among particular subgroups. For example, we might expect a greater increase in the likelihood of obtaining atypical jobs among women with a strong attachment to the labor market. Women with more experience may stand to gain more from any general improvements in opportunities for women, compared to women with minimal or disjointed work histories. Women with greater work experience are likely to have more contacts and be taken more seriously by employers.

Determinants of Occupational Atypicality

To understand better the reasons for previous trends in sex segregation as well as prospects for the future, we need to consider past and possible future changes in those factors that lead many women to choose or to be channeled into so-called women's occupations. The language used to describe these occupations, the term *women's* itself, is a powerful channeling tool, one of several operating so obviously that they can escape scrutiny. Surprisingly little empirical research has been done on why some women choose atypical jobs but most choose traditional ones. A major purpose of this chapter is to help fill this void.

A potential explanation for occupational segregation is that because women typically bear the major share of nonmarket family responsibilities, they have more constraints than men on the time and energy they can give to the labor market. Having less time to develop labor-market skills, they may choose different types of jobs than men.

Operating within a human-capital perspective, Polachek (1979) argues that occupational segregation can be explained at least partly by sex differences in labor-market commitment. He maintains that jobs vary according to how much their required skills atrophy during labor-market interruptions and how much penalty is assigned to intermittent labor-market behavior. According to Polachek, individuals with a weak commitment to the labor market would tend to choose those occupations in which intermittent labor-market behavior is not penalized. Since women are much more likely than men to have a weak commitment to the labor market, it is reasonable to expect them to be concentrated in certain types of occupations, presumably those in which intermittent labor-market behavior is penalized least.

Traditionally, the division of labor within the family calls for women to subordinate their work careers to those of their husbands, so that although men may move to improved job opportunities in different localities, women are more likely to leave their own jobs because of their husbands' job-related move. Further, some so-called women's occupations, such as teaching, are thought to provide the worker with greater control over the hours worked, so that, presumably, it is easier to coordinate day-to-day responsibilities in the home and the work place. This idea has also been used to explain the tendency for women to be concentrated in certain subcategories within male-typed occupations, so that women doctors and lawyers work for the government (Kosa and Coker 1965), women dentists treat primarily children (Shuval 1970), and women engineers teach (Perrucci 1970). These subcategories are thought to allow greater freedom to coordinate work and family responsibilities.

A central point of the arguments discussed so far is that occupational segregation is produced by individual men and women choosing different occupations because of different constraints due to differences in family responsibilities and labor-market commitment.[1] These arguments imply that women with fewer family responsibilities and strong labor-market commitment will be more likely to be in atypical occupations.

To the extent that occupational segregation is not explained by family constraints and labor-market commitment, alternative explanations are needed. Occupational choice may arise, for example, from personality preferences. Early sex-role socialization may cause women to prefer the occupations in which most of them are found, regardless of their family situations or commitment to work. Occupations where women are concentrated generally permit women to act out their socialization toward nurturance and dependence.

Other more current factors may also affect women's occupational choices. Their current perceptions that their chances for success in atypical occupations are lower may lead them to choose female-typed occupations. They may also feel less comfortable in work settings dominated by men, a factor that causes many women to leave atypical occupations after entering them (Kanter 1977). All these factors may lead women to choose typical women's occupations.

Of course, occupational segregation is not entirely (perhaps not even largely) the result of choices made by individual women. Discrimination also contributes to the persistence of occupational segregation; women may simply be excluded from many male occupations. Barriers to women may be found in employer's tastes for hiring men for certain jobs (Becker 1971). Roadblocks for women may also result from statistical discrimination whereby employers attribute to all women certain feminine characteristics (for example, soft, passive, weak labor-market commitment) deemed inappropriate for many male occupations. These barriers often become institutionalized into the hiring and promotion practices of organizations (Kanter 1977), where they take on a reality beyond the decisions of individuals. Another barrier arises from the structure of informal networks within organizations (Kanter 1977) and differential opportunities for formal and informal job training (Taylor 1980), which limit the opportunities for women to develop the sponsorship and skills necessary for advancement into more rewarding (and usually male-typed) jobs.

Consequences of Occupational Atypicality

As noted above, being in a female-typed job significantly lowers earnings for women—and men—even after controlling for individual human-capital factors (Jusenius 1976) and occupational skill requirements (McLaughlin 1978). We will explore this issue further with our sample of middle-aged women, focusing on whether the increased earnings from occupational atypicality have declined over the ten-year period. We will also examine the extent to which the size of this effect differs for women with various levels of work experience.

Method of Analysis

We use regression analysis to examine the effects of calendar time, family constraints, labor-market commitment, and other explanatory variables on atypicality, and then the effects of atypicality on earnings, controlling for the other explanatory variables. Atypicality is measured by the degree to which the respondent's occupation is not a typical occupation for women.[2] We attempt to explain the dependent variables with several groups of independent variables. Human-capital accumulation and labor-market commitment are measured by education, postschool labor-market experience, hours worked in the current year, and job tenure. Family constraints are measured by marital status, number and ages of children, and (as a more general indicator of traditional family orientation) the woman's attitudes toward the appropriateness of married women working. Atypicality is used as a measure of occupational segregation in the equations predicting earnings. To estimate the effect of time on women's labor-market attainment, we have constructed a trend variable. Other variables are included in our equations as basic controls for family background and location of residence.

To analyze the impact of these variables on earnings and atypicality, we organized the data into a pooled cross-section time-series file. The data for most of the analysis came from the 1967, 1972, and 1977 survey years. The file included an observation for each individual for each of these years in which she was interviewed; that is, each interview for each individual was treated as a separate observation. Thus the data file can include as many as three observations (or cases) for each individual. Observations were included if the respondent was employed, reported hourly earnings of at least $.50, and did not have missing data on any of the variables included in the equations.

Most of the variables indicating labor-market commitment and family constraints change over the life cycle. For example, as a woman ages one year, either her number of years worked or her number of years not worked is increased by one. Thus our problem is to distinguish such age or life-cycle effects on atypicality from effects associated with changes in social or labor-market conditions over time (that is, temporal or period effects). Hence, we face the classic problem, discussed extensively in demographic literature, of separating age, period, and cohort effects. Because temporal, life cycle, and cohort effects are linearly dependent, any one effect can be redefined as a combination of the other two. The task is to employ the least restrictive and conceptually appropriate constraints.[3] In the analysis, life-cycle and temporal effects will be identified by assuming that they are additive and cohort effects not accounted for by other variables are negligible.[4] These assumptions are fairly reasonable because we control for several factors that might produce a cohort effect, and all of the members of the sample were born within a 15-year period.

We used ordinary least squares to estimate equations for the basic sample and selected subsamples.[5] In order to investigate whether the processes varied depending on the degree of attachment to the labor market, we estimated the equations for a subsample who had weak labor-market attachment (those who worked twenty-six weeks or more in no more than one-third of the years since leaving school) and for a subsample with strong attachment (who worked twenty-six weeks or more in at least 70 percent of the years since leaving school).

We were also concerned that these processes might differ for black and white women and for women in blue-collar and white-collar occupations. Because attainment processes differ markedly among these different groups of women, many of the analyses were performed separately for each group.

Results

Changes in Atypicality

We first consider changes in atypicality over the decade. Looking at gross percentages (table 4–1) we see a slight increase in the percentage of both black and white women in atypical occupations. Atypicality appears to increase mostly among women in professional or technical occupations, though some increase is also evident among clerical and sales workers and craftswomen. In contrast, the proportion of women in atypical jobs decreased among operatives. Overall, the situation did not improve much for these women over the decade.

Table 4–1
Proportion of Women in Atypical Occupations in 1967 and 1977, by One-Digit Occupation

	Whites		Blacks	
One-Digit Occupation	1967	1977	1967	1977
Professional, technical workers	20	26	9	11
Manager, official, proprietor	99	99	a	100
Clerical and kindred workers	4	5	9	12
Sales	4	13	a	a
Craftsmen, foremen	82	88	a	a
Operatives and kindred workers	47	38	52	43
Private household workers	0	0	0	0
Service workers	4	4	4	5
Total	21	23	19	20
Sample size	2037	1790	1040	696

Note: Typical female three-digit occupations in each of the one-digit categories are: teacher, department store head, secretary, sales clerk, bookbinder, sewer, housekeeper, waitress; male-typed jobs are: engineer, manager, shipping clerk, insurance salesman, foreman, welder, bartender. No private-household occupation is predominantly male.

[a]Percentage not shown when sample size less than 20.

The regression results provide an estimate of the amount of change associated with calendar time, net of women's human capital and family constraints. The equations predicting atypicality, presented in table 4-2, include indicators of family constraints, human capital, and calendar time as well as some basic controls. The trend variable in our model is designed to capture the effects on occupational structure and labor-market opportunities over calendar time net of changes over the life cycle. For whites, the effect of the trend variable on atypicality is small and insignificant, suggesting no change in the structure of occupational sex segregation among

Table 4-2
Atypicality of Occupation: Regression Results by Race

Explanatory Variables	Whites (1)	Whites (2)	Blacks (1)	Blacks (2)
Calendar time				
Trend	− .026	.099	.588**	.359
Family Constraints				
Married, spouse present	− .444	− .364	1.550	1.010
Number of children				
less than 6 years old	1.110	1.110	− .358	.415
between 6 and 17 years	.090	.208	.464	.485
older than 17 years	.665	.750	− 1.340	− 1.600†
Sex-role attitudes	− .055	− .055	.277	.274
Human Capital and Labor-Market Commitment				
Education				
8 years or less		10.800**		− 4.510*
9–11 years		7.850**		− 2.080
13–15 years		− 4.310**		− 3.320
16 years or more		3.220*		3.350
Age	.173		− .192	
Years worked since school		− 2.330		1.560
Years not worked since school		.519		5.960†
Hours worked last year		− 7.040		2.990**
Tenure on current job		9.630**		− 6.000*
$\bar{R}^2$	.00	.03	.01	.02
Sample size	3864	3864	1641	1641

Note: The results include controls for health, residence in the South, residence in an SMSA, size of local labor force, local unemployment rate, mother's atypicality, whether mother worked, and father's occupational status. Complete regression equations are available from the Center for Human Resource Research on request.

**Significant at .01 level.
*Significant at .05 level.
†Significant at .10 level.

middle-aged women between 1967 and 1977. For blacks, the trend term is positive and significant in equation 1 but becomes insignificant when the human-capital variables are included in equation 2, indicating that changes in human capital account for the small increase in atypicality that did take place. These results are in general agreement with previous studies finding little or no change (Blau and Hendricks 1979; Beller 1980; England 1980).

To be sure, the 1967–1977 period was one of generally declining economic and labor-market conditions. Since unfavorable labor-market conditions are generally associated with lower opportunities for women and minorities, there might have been some structural change had labor-market conditions been more favorable. To examine this possibility, we repeated the analysis including the national unemployment rate for the year of interview as an explanatory variable.[6] When the unemployment-rate variable was included, it turned out negative, but small and insignificant, and the trend coefficient showed a small but insignificant increase. This further analysis indicates that the lack of change in occupational sex segregation should not be attributed to stagnant economic conditions. This lack of change toward a broader range of occupations was observed during a period of major changes in labor-force participation among women and attitudes toward women working; the persistence of occupational segregation in the face of these other changes implies a need to better understand determinants of occupational atypicality among women, a subject to which we now turn.

Causes of Atypicality

The results for the first equation in table 4–2 allow us to examine the total effects of family constraints, effects that may operate directly or indirectly through human-capital accumulation and labor-market commitment. The second equation also includes measures of human-capital accumulation and labor-market commitment, allowing us to examine direct effects. For both blacks and whites, contrary to theoretical expectations, family constraints have little effect on atypicality, either directly or indirectly. This lack of effect contrasts sharply with the effects of family constraints on hourly earnings (table 4–3), where we see results more consistent with sociological and economic theory: the greater the number of children a woman has, the lower her pay. A women who subscribes to the traditional attitude that her family responsibilities take precedence over her work has lower pay as well. Also consistent with these theories is that nearly half of the effect of sex-role attitudes and virtually all of the effects of children on earnings operate through human-capital accumulation and labor-market commitment.

For whites, the effects of education on atypicality are curvilinear (table 4–2). Controlling for other factors, we find that women with less than

Table 4–3
(Log) Hourly Earnings: Regression Results by Race

Explanatory Variables	Whites		Blacks	
	(1)	*(2)*	*(1)*	*(2)*
Atypicality		.001**		.003**
Family Constraints				
Married, spouse present	− .016	.053**	.075**	.035†
Number of children				
less than 6 years old	− .022	.001	− .048**	− .016
between 6 and 17 years	− .037**	− .003	− .033**	.004
older than 17 years	− .030**	− .004	− .016	.013
Sex-role attitudes	.022**	.009**	.129**	.007†
Human Capital and Labor-Market Commitment				
Education				
8 years or less		− .215**		− .291**
9–11 years		− .215**		− .140**
13–15 years		.141**		.188**
16 years or more		.293**		.625**
Age	.002		− .009**	
Years worked since school		.088*		.092
Years not worked since school		− .198**		− .082†
Hours worked last year		.067**		.019
Tenure at current job		.278**		.098*
$\bar{R}^2$	.14	.34	.32	.55
Sample size	3864	3864	1641	1641

Note: The results include controls for health, residence in the South, residence in an SMSA, size of local labor force, local unemployment rate, mother's atypicality, whether mother worked, and father's occupational status. Complete regression equations are available from the Center for Human Resource Research on request.
**Significant at .01 level.
*Significant at .05 level.
†Significant at .10 level.

twelve years of education are the most likely to be in atypical occupations; those with twelve to fifteen years are least likely to be in atypical occupations; and college graduates are in between.[7] This finding is consistent with the notion that, although female-typed jobs tend not to be the most powerful and highest paying, they also tend not to be the most undesirable of the jobs available to women. Alternatively, barriers to women may simply be stronger in higher prestige occupations. For blacks, education effects on atypicality tend to be smaller and less systematic, although there seems to be a slight tendency for women with more education to be in less typical occupations.

Human-capital theory would predict that the number of years of work experience, hours worked in the previous year, and tenure with current employer would have positive effects on atypicality and that years of not working would have a negative effect. However, in each equation only one of these four variables is significant in the predicted direction. Again, this result contrasts with the results for the effect of years worked, hours, tenure, and years not worked on hourly earnings; there, all of the effects are in the predicted direction, although three of the four are not statistically significant for blacks.[8] More generally, the very low R^2s for the atypicality equations (.03 for whites and .02 for blacks) indicate that occupational segregation is not accounted for by differences in family constraints and labor-market commitment. These results contradict Polachek's (1979) hypothesis derived from human-capital theory.[9]

To illustrate, let us consider two hypothetical white women who have twenty-five years of postschool experience and are identical in all characteristics except labor-market commitment. Let us suppose that, like the prototypical man, women A is strongly committed to the labor market as indicated by having twenty-five years of postschool work experience, no years in which she did not work, and 2,000 hours of employment in the previous year; in addition, she has been with her present employer for seven years. Let us also suppose that, like many women with family respon- sibilities, woman B has a weaker commitment to the labor market as in- dicated by having ten years of postschool work experience, 15 years in which she did not work outside the home, 1,000 hours of employment in the previous year, and only one year with her present employer. Using equation 2 in table 4–2, we find that the expected atypicality for woman A is 2.1 greater than the atypicality for women B: that is, we expect a 2 percentage point difference in atypicality between two white women with radically dif- ferent degrees of labor-market commitment. If our hypothetical women are black, the expected atypicality is actually lower, by 3.6 percentage points, for the woman with the stronger labor-market commitment. This com- parison strongly suggests that occupational sex segregation has little to do with individuals choosing different occupations because of their degree of commitment to the labor market. Thus, the persistent sex segregation in the labor market might not be alleviated much by attempts to increase women's work commitment or to reduce their family involvement.

Consequences of Atypicality for Women's Earnings

To examine the effect of atypicality on earnings, we consider the results from the earnings equation (table 4–3). The coefficient for atypicality is positive and statistically significant for both whites and blacks. The magnitude of the coefficients implies that, net of individual characteristics, being in an occupation that is 90-percent male instead of one that is 90-percent female brings about 8 and 20 percent higher hourly earnings for whites and blacks, respectively.

In order to test whether the effect of atypicality on earnings may have changed over the period, we also ran the model including an atypicality-by-trend multiplicative interaction term. Although not shown here, the coefficients on this term were small and insignificant, indicating that the impact of atypicality on hourly earnings did not change during this period.

Differences across Occupation and
Labor-Market Commitment

When the atypicality equations were run separately for women in white-collar and blue-collar occupations,[10] both sets of results were similar to those presented above: family constraints and labor-market commitment had small and usually insignificant effects on atypicality, and little if any change in atypicality appeared over calendar time net of life-cycle effects. However, we did find dramatic differences between white- and blue-collar occupations in the size of the effect of atypicality on earnings. For both whites and blacks, being in a 90-percent male occupation instead of a 90-percent female occupation brings less than 1 percent higher earnings for white-collar jobs, but 32 percent higher earnings for blue-collar jobs. In addition, the similarity in the size of the effects for whites and blacks suggests that the racial differences in the effects of atypicality on earnings noted above (table 4–3) are not due to race per se but to the differential representation of whites and blacks in white- and blue-collar occupations.

As discussed already, we might expect women who exhibit a continuous commitment to the labor market to be the primary beneficiaries of improved opportunities. To examine this issue, we reestimated our equations for atypicality and earnings for two subsamples of women: (1) those exhibiting a high degree of commitment to the labor market (that is, worked twenty-six or more weeks in at least 70 percent of the years since leaving school); and (2) those exhibiting a low degree of commitment (that is, worked twenty-six or more weeks in no more than one-third of the years since leaving school).[11] For whites, the trend in earnings conformed to our expectations: controlling for labor-market experience, education and other individual characteristics, the earnings of women with a strong commitment to the labor market increased slightly during the period, while the earnings of women with a weak commitment decreased slightly. However, earnings increased for blacks in both groups, but larger increases occurred among those with the lowest labor-market commitment. Furthermore, the trend in atypicality did not conform to our expectations. For both whites and blacks, women who were strongly committed to the labor market were less likely to move into atypical occupations than were those with a weak commitment, although the differences between the two groups were not statistically significant.

Conclusions

We found both confirmation and contradictions of current ideas about occupational sex segregation. First, our results support those of several previous studies in that we found little or no change in the tendency for middle-aged women to be in female-typed occupations. Our results also suggest that this lack of change was not attributable to the stagnant economic conditions prevailing during the 1970s. Hence, equal employment opportunity efforts on the part of the federal government have apparently not been successful in helping middle-aged women to move into a broader range of occupations, although it should be noted that our results may be peculiar to the age group of women under investigation. We might expect to find more change in a sample that included women of all ages; younger women who entered the labor force during the decade may have been more likely to choose atypical occupations.

Our results are in general agreement with those of Jusenius (1976); we found that being in a female-typed job had a very large detrimental impact on the hourly earnings of women in blue-collar occupations but no effect on the earnings of women in white-collar occupations. Whatever the social perception of female-typed jobs in the white-collar sector (that is, secretaries, nurses, teachers), women in these occupations are not underpaid compared to women in atypical white-collar occupations. Of course, to assess the full impact of sex segregation, we must compare women with men of the same age and work experience in these occupations, which is not possible with our data. In addition, it may be the case that for younger women, who are entering higher status white-collar occupations in increasing numbers, employment in an atypical occupation may indeed be rewarded with higher earnings.

Perhaps the most important findings were those concerning the different ways that family constraints and labor-market commitment affect earnings and atypicality. Their estimated effects on earnings were consistent with economic and sociological theories that emphasize the detrimental effects of family constraints on the time and energy most women spend in market work. In general, indicators of family responsibilities had negative and significant effects on earnings, and most of these effects operated through the strong effects of the labor-market-commitment variables.

Taken together, variation in family responsibilities, human-capital accumulation, and labor-market commitment explained a significant portion of the variation in earnings. (However, a substantial portion of the variation in earnings was left unexplained, implying that other factors, such as labor-market discrimination, are also at work).

In contrast, theories that emphasize family constraints on the time and energies of women do not explain the differential allocation of women to male- and female-typed occupations. Among whites, those who displayed a strong commitment to the labor market were only very slightly more likely than women with a weak commitment to be in atypical or male-typed occupations; moreover, among blacks, those who displayed a strong commitment to the labor market were actually slightly more likely to be in female-typed occupations. Our results thus contradict the hypothesis, derived from human-capital theory by Polachek (1979), that occupational sex segregation is largely explained by men and women choosing different occupations based on differences in their commitment to the labor market.

What do these results suggest for potential future changes in sexual inequality? They imply that reducing the family responsibilities of women—by increasing day-care facilities or fundamentally changing the traditional gender-based division of labor within the family—will improve women's earnings opportunities, but reducing family responsibilities alone would have little impact on occupational sex segregation, at least for women in this age group. The tendency to be in female-typed occupations is probably due to a combination of factors including discriminatory employment practices by firms that place hurdles, and sometimes even barriers, to women entering nontraditional occupations; the awareness by women of this discrimination, which may discourage many from considering these occupations in the first place; and early socialization influences that lead women to prefer female-typed occupations in an effort to reduce the conflict or maximize the consistency between work roles and more general social roles based on gender.

Notes

1. However, there may be substantial disagreement among the proponents of these arguments as to the "appropriateness" of the traditional sex-role division of labor in the home that produces these different constraints, as well as differences over whether division of labor should be viewed as a free choice made by men and women or viewed as resulting from broader restrictions on the opportunities of women.

2. More specifically, atypicality is measured by the percentage of the incumbents of the respondent's occupation who are men minus the percent-

age of individuals in the civilian labor force who are men (Jusenius 1976). Atypicality is coded at the three-digit 1960 census-code level and is based on the 1970 occupational distribution.

3. There is a rather extensive literature on possible solutions to this problem. See, for example, Pullman (1978), Winsborough (1975), Winsborough and Duncan (forthcoming).

4. That is, we assume that any overall cohort effect will be captured by differences across cohorts in the average level of individual characteristics included in the model, such as mother's and father's occupation, education, and location of residence.

5. In a pooled data set such as this, it is unreasonable to believe that there is no association among the residual terms within individuals. When such association exists, our procedure of using ordinary least squares (OLS) is not maximally efficient and provides biased estimates, in an unknown direction, of the standard errors of the parameters. Nonetheless, this procedure was used because it provides unbiased estimates of the parameters, and previous experience suggests that there are only small differences in the parameters estimated by OLS and a more efficient error-components procedure.

6. For this analysis it was necessary to use all the interview years between 1967 and 1977 because the trend in the unemployment rate was almost linear when only 1967, 1972, and 1977 were used (3.8, 5.6, and 7.0, respectively): thus the trend variable and the unemployment-rate variable would be almost perfectly collinear and their separate effects could not be distinguished. However, when the other years were included, the change in the unemployment rate was not monotonic throughout this period: it fell a little in the late 1960s, rose at the beginning of the 1970s, fell in 1973, and then rose to a peak in 1975. Since sex-role attitudes were only measured in selected years, this variable was dropped from this portion of the analysis.

7. The pattern of the education effects was not changed significantly when the equation was run without the labor-market-experience variables (years worked since school, years not worked since school, hours worked last year, and tenure on current job).

8. It is interesting to note that the effect of years not worked on earnings is negative and (at least for whites) significant, a finding that supports the general conclusions of Mincer and Polachek (1974), Suter and Miller (1973), and Treiman and Terrell (1975) but not those of Corcoran (1979b) and Shaw, chapter 2, this book.

9. We were concerned that our results may be sensitive to our choice of a continuous metric for atypicality, that the fine distinctions made here may not be as accurate (or important) as the simple distinction between an occupation being atypical or typical. Thus, we also ran the regressions with atypicality measured as a dichotomous variable. The explanatory power

(R^2 = .03 for whites and .01 for blacks) of the variables in these alternative regressions and the pattern of the parameter values were similar to those in table 4-2. Perhaps the most significant difference was that for whites the effect of nonworking experience became negative and marginally significant while the statisical significance of the effect of tenure was reduced. A standardization analogous to the one in the text for our two hypothetical women revealed that the expected probability of the woman with the strong commitment to the labor market to be in an atypical occupation was only .01 higher than the expected probability for the woman with a weak commitment.

10. Professionals, managers, sales workers, and clerical workers were classified as *white collar*. Craftsmen, operatives, laborers, service workers, and farm workers were classified as *blue collar*.

11. We were concerned that any differences between these two samples may reflect life-cycle differences as well as more enduring differences in labor-market commitment. This confounding effect of life-cycle differences might occur if younger women are overrepresented in the weak-commitment sample simply because we are more likely to be observing them in their childrearing years. To examine this possibility, we considered selected characteristics of women with attachment to the labor force, as well as—for comparative purposes—a group of women with intermediate attachment to the labor force (women who worked between 70 percent and 33 percent of the years since leaving school). There are virtually no differences in age, length of time since school, and education among these groups. However, these three groups of women are different in their traditional family involvements. Women with strong labor-force attachment were less likely to be married and have had children than women with less work experience. When they did have children, women with a strong attachment tended to have, on average, at least one less child than the other women and, because of this, their youngest child tended to be older. It seems, then, that these differences in labor-force attachment do not reflect life-cycle stage (age, time since school) but rather reflect differential attachments to traditional family life, which are, in turn, related to labor-force commitment. Women with weak or intermittent attachment have more family commitments (husbands, more children, younger children) that might constrain their labor-force involvement.

5

Attitudes toward Women Working: Changes over Time and Implications for the Labor-Force Behaviors of Husbands and Wives

Anne Statham and
Patricia Rhoton

Because women's attitudes have been changing as dramatically as their labor-force participation, this chapter examines the relationship between attitudes and work activity. Many researchers find that liberalized attitudes toward working women are important determinants of women's increasing propensity to work. Women who approve of women working are more likely to desire future employment (Waite and Stolzenberg 1976), to be employed at any one point in time (Dowdall 1974; Mason and Bumpass 1975; Sampson, Dunsing, and Hafstrom 1975; Ferree 1979; Scanzoni 1977) and to participate in the labor force more continuously (Kim and Murphy 1973; Spitze and Spaeth 1976; Macke, Hudis, and Larrick 1978).

However, work experience also has an impact on attitudes. Prior research has produced quite clear evidence that women's experiences in the labor market affect their attitudes toward women working, increasing their propensity to endorse women's employment even more. Thus an important feedback effect, whereby a woman's approval of women working and her own work experience continuously reinforce each other through time, may cause both to increase at a greater rate than might otherwise be expected (Macke, Hudis, and Larrick 1978). To the extent that this feedback occurs, projections of women's labor-force participation must take changes in attitudes into account. Indeed, some prior research shows that aggregate-level projections of trends in female employment patterns are substantially improved by incorporating aggregate measures of attitude shifts (Waite 1979).

This chapter considers the relationship between attitudes toward women working and women's work activity over time. Prior work has found feedback effects between labor-force participation and attitudes toward work for women between 1967 and 1972 (Macke, Hudis, and Larrick 1978; Ferree 1979). Here we replicate this work, then consider these same relationships over the next five-year interval, 1972 to 1977, in order to make use of information for the full decade. Our model, which is depicted schematically in figure 5-1, reflects the ideas that, controlling for one's prior propensity to be in the labor force, attitudes toward women working will affect subsequent work activity and a higher level of work activity, whether it results from nontraditional attitudes or from other sources, may have a significant effect on subsequent attitudes. Women with more work experience may come to approve of women working even more than they originally did. They may enjoy the experience of working, the income that it provides, and/or come to realize that it need not be harmful to family relationships.

Past research has also considered the impact of the husband's attitudes as well as the woman's own attitudes on her work activity. Most women, especially those in this age group, do not form their attitudes or make decisions about working (Mortimer and Lorence 1979; Centers, Raven, and Rodrigues 1971) or about work-related human-capital accumulation (Spitze and Spaeth 1976) without considering the attitudes of their husbands. In fact, the husband's feelings about his wife's working may actually have more impact on her work behavior than the woman's own preferences or orientations (Macke, Hudis, and Larrick 1978; Chenoweth and Maret 1980). Since the majority of women in this age group—age 30–44 in 1967— are married, their husbands' influence must be considered in any account of their work attitudes and behaviors.

One earlier study (Macke, Hudis, and Larrick 1978) considered the

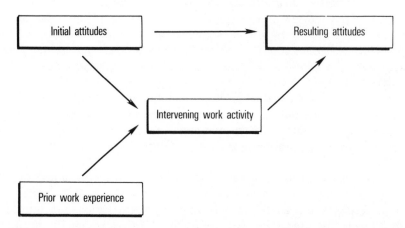

Figure 5-1. Model of Relationship between Work Activity and Attitudes toward Work

impact of the husband's attitudes on a woman's work activity, but it looked at the wife's perceptions of her husband's attitudes as an indicator of how the husband actually felt. Here we also consider not only the impact of the wife's perception of the husband's views but, in addition, we also have measures of the husband's actual attitudes toward women working. A special subset of the mature women's cohort were married to respondents in the NLS older men's cohort and, for this subset, we can substitute the husband's actual attitudes for the wife's perceptions of his attitudes and compare the two effects.

The model presented in figure 5-2 is an expansion of that presented in figure 5-1. It asserts that the husband's actual attitudes influence the woman's work activity, as past research has shown to be true of the woman's perception of those attitudes (Macke, Hudis, and Larrick 1978; Chenoweth and Maret 1980). It also asserts that the husband's attitudes are influenced by the woman's work activity, an argument that also receives some support from past research. Women at least perceive that their work activity affects their husbands' attitudes (Spitze and Waite 1981); other research shows that husbands' attitudes are affected over time by their wives' attitudes (Cronkite 1977). However, the direct impact of the wife's labor-force behavior on the husband's actual attitudes remains to be examined. The issue has critical implications: if husbands' attitudes are an important restrictor of women's labor-force participation, current increases in employment might relax this restrictor, resulting in a spiraling upward increase in employment that could not be anticipated from current conditions.

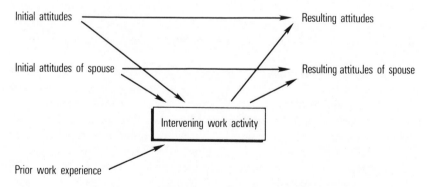

Figure 5-2. Proposed Model for Attitude Change

Implications for Husbands' Work Activity

The model in figure 5-2 also can be used to test whether men's attitudes toward women working may affect their own work activity as well as that of their wives. To be sure, because the husbands in the subsample were aged 56–70 and either retired or nearing retirement at the time of the 1977 interview, conclusions about their work activity should be made with caution. However, if both husbands and wives increase their approval of women working, gender-based decisions about family responsibilities may change, in turn altering men's work activity. Specifically, changed perceptions of responsibility for the family's financial support may evolve; some recent evidence suggests that increasing approval for and higher levels of women's work activity results in husbands and wives perceiving financial support as a shared responsibility (Macke 1978; Statham 1980; Statham and Larrick 1980). If so, husbands in younger age groups than those in our sample may also be affected by these forces: they may feel less pressure to participate continuously in the labor force and they may actually work less than more traditional husbands. Their own lower work activity, along with their wives' increased activity, may increase their nontraditional attitudes even more, resulting in the same feedback effect predicted for the women.

Analytic Strategy

Data

To estimate the models implied in figure 5-2, we will use two samples. First, we will attempt to replicate past work across the entire ten-year interval with the full NLS cohort, limiting the analysis to women married to the same spouse throughout the decade. Models estimated with this larger sample use only the woman's perceptions of her husband's attitudes as indicators of his attitudes.

To estimate models that incorporate the husband's actual attitudes and his work activity, we use the smaller sample of women for whom information is also available from husbands. Thanks to the procedure involved in drawing the sample of 5,000 women aged 30–44 in 1967 and 5,000 men aged 45–59 in 1966, both spouses in approximately 375 families were interviewed in the initial years of the NLS. A combination of sample attrition, marital disruption due to death or divorce, or noninterview of one or both of the spouses in a critical year reduced this original group to 285 couples by 1977. However, for these couples we have complete attitudinal and employment information at several points in time across the ten-year interval, a truly rare opportunity.

Enthusiasm for this data set should be tempered by the realization that the same sampling procedure that produced it makes its generalizability questionable. Not all the husbands of wives in the original women's sample were included: only the husbands who were aged 45–59 in 1966. Thus, the average age difference between the spouses in the sample is eight years, somewhat wider than that in the population as a whole, and this age difference may be especially problematic for the issue we wish to examine. Older husbands tend to have more power in marriages, so the husbands in our sample may have more than usual power in the marital relationship, resulting in a possible overstatement of the impact of husbands' attitudes. To test this possibility, the model used for all married women is reestimated for this special subset. If the husbands in this smaller sample are indeed more powerful, the impact of the woman's perceptions of her husband's attitudes on her work activity should be considerably larger than the effect found in the larger sample of women. To test for other possible sample differences, we compared both samples on standard socioeconomic and attitudinal indices. Overall, we found the husbands and wives in this subsample to be remarkably similar to the husbands and wives from the original 5,000 who remained married over this time interval.

Variables

In the models outlined already, attitudes toward women working were usually measured by a three-item scale asking the respondents' attitudes toward married women working under three conditions: if it is economically necessary, if the husband agrees, and if the husband disagrees.[1] To simplify the analysis, responses to these items, which ranged on a five-point scale from strongly agree to strongly disagree, were summed. Doing so increased the reliability of the attitude measures and improved the estimate of the true relationships between these variables. Though the three items are so different that one might suspect them to be differentially related to labor-force participation, many of the models estimated below were redone using the items separately, with no substantial changes in the results.

These three items were available for the women in 1967, 1972, and 1977 and for the men in the husband and wife subsample in 1971. A single-item measure was available for the men in this subsample in 1967: it asked the men to choose one of five conditions under which it would be appropriate for married women to work.[2] Though the single item and three-item measures are not strictly comparable, the correlation between them (.218) is significant in the husband/wife sample and nearly as high as that between identical items measured for the women at different time points (approximately .300). Unfortunately, no attitudinal measures were available for the men beyond 1971, a fact that constrains the analyses for the husband/wife subsample. Because of this limitation, we estimate models in this subsample for 1967 to 1971–1972, as we have attitudinal measures for both husbands and wives in 1967 and 1971–1972; when we estimate the model for the second five-year interval, 1972 to 1977, and for the entire ten-year interval, we use only the women's attitudes as 1977 outcomes. Results for the two five-year intervals as well as for the entire decade will show any changes in the processes over time. Unfortunately, we will have less information about the effect of work activity on the husband's attitudes than on the attitudes of the wives.

The woman's perception of her husband's attitude is measured by a single item that asks the woman how her husband does (or would) feel about her working (or starting to work).[3] This measure, available in 1967 and 1972, is not strictly comparable to the husbands' attitudinal measure because the husband is asked how he feels about married women working in general, not about his wife in particular. However, the two measures are significantly correlated in the husband/wife subsample. (The correlations range from .319 to .257.)

Work activity was measured by restricting the measures to behaviors occurring between the two time points and calculating the number of weeks worked over the three time intervals. For instance, to calculate weeks worked by the women between 1967 and 1972, we only considered weeks worked after the 1967 interview and before the 1972 interview. We did not wish to include labor-market activity that occurred at the same time the attitudes were measured since reciprocal causation would be more of a problem in that case. Similar procedures were used to construct weeks-worked variables for the men in the husband/wife subsample.

To estimate these effects, several control variables were used, including the respondent's age, race, and educational attainment in 1967. We controlled for the existence of health problems, the Duncan index of the respondent's current or last job, work experience, and family constraints. Because men's and women's experiences in these areas are so different, we used different measures for the two sexes in the analysis of the husband/wife subsample. In terms of work experience, the relevant factor for women is whether or not they have worked at all. Thus we controlled for women's employment status in 1967 (or 1972), a known correlate of past work experience (Heckman 1979).[4] Since men are likely to have worked fairly consistently throughout their lives, the length of time on their present job is perhaps a more valid indicator of the amount of work activity or of other factors which might confound our results, so we controlled for their job tenure in 1967.

The controls for family constraints were devised in keeping with traditional family-role obligations. Women feel pressured to remain at home with young children, so their work activity may be most constrained by the age of their youngest child (Sweet 1973). Thus we controlled for the age of the women's youngest child in 1967. Men's work activity may be more constrained by their traditional responsibilities for financial support, which might be better indicated by the number of dependents they have than by the age of their youngest child. Hence, number of children in 1967 was used as a control for the men. We also controlled for spouses' average income over the relevant time interval, again being careful to exclude values that overlapped the measurement of attitudes.

Variables likely to remain constant in value (race) or in effect (age) through time were assigned the same value throughout the analysis. Others that tended to change more, such as health problems, work activity, job tenure, occupational prestige (*Duncan index*), age of youngest child, and spouse's income, were assigned different values depending on the interval being considered.[5]

Because of the limited size of the husband/wife subsample, we cannot reliably estimate the full regression models separately by race. For the sake of comparability, however, we conducted the entire analysis with blacks and whites combined, adding race as a control variable.

Effects of Wives' Attitudes and Perceptions of their Husbands' Attitudes on Wives' Work Activity

Results for the Full Sample

Results of the regression analyses of the effects of wives' own attitudes and their perception of husbands' attitudes on their work activity as well as the effects of work activity on attitudes are presented in figure 5-3.[6] Past research suggested that the impact of attitudes on work activity was significant but not as great as the impact of work activity on subsequent attitudes (Macke, Hudis, and Larrick 1978). This pattern is also found here, and by the last five years of the decade, the impact of attitudes on work activity is only barely significant. Hence, it appears that, over time, the impact of work activity on subsequent attitudes has become even more important, relative to the impact of attitudes on subsequent work activity. The importance of the woman's perception of her husband's attitudes for her work activity has not declined appreciably through time, however. As past research shows, these perceptions are a much more important determinant of the woman's work activity than her own attitudes toward women working.

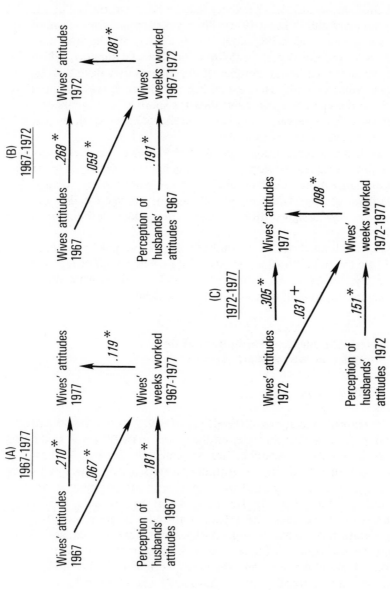

Figure 5–3. Wives' Weeks Worked as Determinant and Consequence of Wives' Attitudes and Wives' Perceptions of Husbands' Attitudes: All Women from NLS Cohort Married throughout Decade (Standardized Coefficients)

Results for the Husband/Wife Subsample

Results for models including perceptions of husbands' attitudes for this subsample are presented in figure 5-4. The tendency for the impact of work activity on subsequent attitudes to become relatively more important across time appears in this subsample as well as in the full NLS sample. Although both samples showed a lessening effect of attitudes on subsequent work activity between the first and second five-year periods, the decline was much greater in the husband/wife sample: in fact, by 1972–1977 attitudes no longer had a significant effect on work activity in this group. This decline could represent a general lessening of the importance of women's attitudes for their work activity as favorable attitudes become more widespread and working becomes commonplace, but the lack of any effect in the husband/ wife sample may also be due to the age of the group. The majority of these women were entering their fifties in the 1972–1977 period. Regardless of their attitudes, by these ages women may not be able to find suitable jobs unless they have substantial work experience.

Contrary to our fears, the impact of perceived husband's attitudes was not greater in the husband/wife subsample. In fact, in 1967–1972, its effect was actually smaller. In general, then, the results from these two samples are reasonably congruent and yield similar substantive conclusions: the impact of attitudes on work activity has decreased over time, while the impact of work activity on attitudes has increased. And perceptions of husband's attitudes remains a strong determinant of a married woman's work activity.

Husbands' Actual Attitudes and Wives' Work Activity

If husbands and wives always agreed on the propriety of women working and if wives always perceived their husbands attitudes correctly, models using only wives' attitudes would be sufficient. However, correlations between husbands' and wives' attitudes show considerable difference between them. In fact, husbands and wives appeared to have more similar attitudes about women working earlier than they did later, as shown by the larger correlations between their attitudes in 1967 than in 1971–1972 (.262 and .039, respectively). This tendency toward more agreement at the first time period was true despite the fact that different questions were asked of women and men in 1967, while the same question was asked of both in 1971–1972. A smaller trend away from husband-wife agreement appears in the correlations between the wives' perceptions of the husbands' attitudes and the husbands' actual attitude measures (.319 and .257). Perhaps some deterioration in husbands' and wives' understanding and agreement

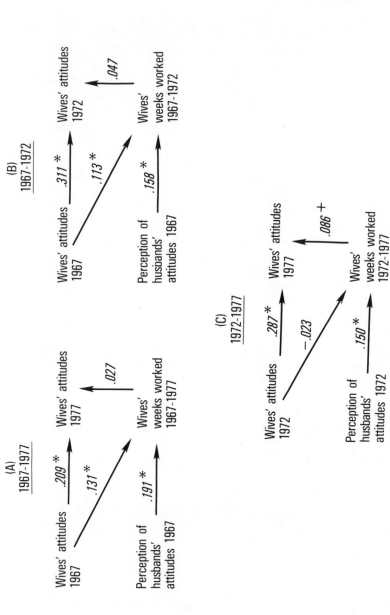

*Significant at the .05 level.
†Significant at the .15 level.

Figure 5–4. Wives' Weeks Worked as Determinant and Consequence of Wives' Attitudes and Perceptions of Husbands' Attitudes: Women in Husband/Wife Subsample (Standardized Coefficients)

occurred over the time interval, though the change in measures makes it difficult to draw this conclusion with any degree of certainty. The fact that the later men's measure is the same as the women's lends some support to the argument that the change is not caused by measurement change, since in that case, the 1971 measure should be more highly correlated with the women's attitudes. The trend may result instead from a widening gap in opinions between the sexes over time, as suggested by other research (Araji 1977; Albrecht, Bohr, and Chadwick 1979).

The correlations between the husbands' attitudes and wives' perceptions of those attitudes tend to be higher than those between the women's attitudes and the men's. At least wives do not seem to be projecting their own attitudes onto their husbands.[7] However, as figure 5-5 shows, husbands' actual attitudes have no impact on their wives' work activity. This total lack of any significant effect is surprising, given the rather strong impact of the woman's perception of her husband's attitudes and the significant correlation between these perceptions and the husband's actual attitudes. Perhaps a husband's feelings about his own wife's working, in particular—not his attitudes about women working in general—constrain her behavior. Alternatively, wives may perceive that their husbands disapprove more than they actually do and that misperception may constrain the women's behaviors.

Husbands' attitudes are related to their wives' work activity in another way, however: they are significantly affected by wives' prior work activity in 1971. Men whose wives participate more fully in the labor force increase their approval of married women working.

Husbands' Work Activity and Attitudes toward Women Working

The fact that these husbands' attitudes are significantly modified by the women's work activity may have implications for the husband's own work activity. The results reported in figure 5-6 show a slight tendency for husbands' own attitudes to affect their own work activity during the second five-year interval (C); less traditional husbands tended to work fewer weeks than more traditional husbands. This effect was even stronger over the entire decade (A); perhaps the impact of a husband's nontraditionality on his own work behavior is stronger over the long run than the short run.

Apparently the men of this sample are beginning to adjust their laborforce behavior to their attitudes toward women working. If this tendency is widespread and not simply peculiar to this sample, it could have important implications for society as a whole—for future work patterns and family roles, in particular. If men begin to feel less compelled toward maximum

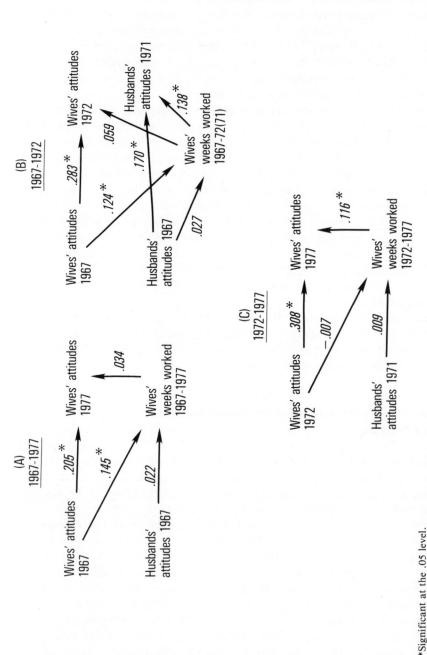

Figure 5–5. Wives' Weeks Worked as Determinant and Consequence of Wives' Attitudes and Husbands' Attitudes: Women in Husband/Wife Subsample (Standardized Coefficients)

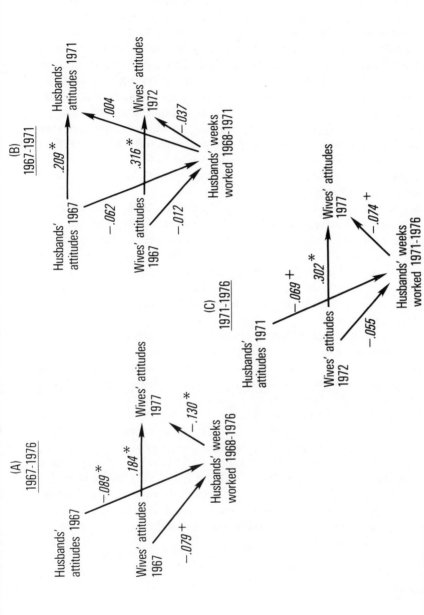

*Significant at the .05 level.
†Significant at the .15 level.

Figure 5–6. Husbands' Weeks Worked as Determinant and Consequence of Husbands' Attitudes and Wives' Attitudes: Men in Husband/Wife Subsample (Standardized Coefficients)

work activity because of changes in women's roles, they may devote more time and attention to family matters. Of course, many other outcomes are possible from reduced weeks in the labor force, but changes in family roles may be most important in terms of women's future labor-force involvement. Family obligations seem to be the most powerful force preventing women's full involvement at the present time. That older men seem to be tapering off their work involvement somewhat in response to attitudes toward women's roles is significant; perhaps they are opting for full or partial early retirement if they do not feel totally responsible for the family's financial support. If family roles are changing in this way, younger men who adopt these newer attitudes may show a propensity to reduce their work activity—periodically or permanently—even before the opportunity for retirement arrives. Some previous research suggests that such a trend may be occurring (Statham 1980).

Since we did not measure husband's attitudes in 1976, we cannot test for the existence of a feedback effect between work activity and attitudes during this second time interval. Possibly, reduced labor-market experience increased these men's propensity to approve of women's employment even more than before. The men's employment pattern began to affect their wives' attitudes during the second half of the interval (again, even more strongly over the entire decade), so it may well have begun to affect their own attitudes.

Over the entire decade, wives whose husbands worked fewer hours increased their endorsement of women's employment. A slight tendency also appears for wives' attitudes to affect their husband's work activity; husbands of nontraditional women are likely to work fewer hours. Hence, a feedback effect across time may have been developing between women's attitudes and their husbands' work activity (rather than with their own activity) toward the end of the interval. If these effects should grow stronger through time, the implications could be quite important, especially considering that women's attitudes are becoming less traditional through time because of their own work activity as well (see figure 5-5). Remember also that husbands' attitudes were modified substantially by their wives' labor-force behaviors. Assuming that all of these indirect influences remain fairly constant through time, they might substantially modify men's work activity over a long period of time.

Conclusions

These results suggest that the feedback between women's work activity and attitudes toward working found in previous research (Macke, Hudis, and Larrick 1978) may be declining through time. While the effect of work activity on attitudes is substantial and may even be getting larger, the

impact of attitudes on work activity is becoming smaller and less significant, even for the full NLS cohort of continuously married women. Of
course, this trend may be peculiar to the age group of women considered
here. Perhaps these women are coming to the age where, if they have not
already begun to work, they can find nothing but undesirable jobs, so they
are unlikely to work regardless of their attitudes. (This would be even more
true of the women in the husband/wife sample since they are at the upper
end of the age distribution.)

Although the dynamic relationship between work activity and attitudes
may be lessening for women, we found evidence that a feedback relationship between women's attitudes and their husbands' work activity may have
begun in the second half of the survey years. In addition, we speculated that
such a feedback system may be developing for the men's own attitudes and
their work activity, though we have no measure of men's attitudes at the
end of the period to test this speculation.

More research is needed to determine whether a relationship between
role attitudes (of both husbands and wives) and men's work activity exists
among younger men as well as among those nearing retirement age. It may
be that men who are looking forward to retirement in any event find sharing
of provider and family roles with their wives easier to contemplate than
younger men who may still feel caught up in conventional achievement patterns. If such a relationship does develop among younger men it may affect
both women's and men's future roles in society. Currently, many working
women feel they must continue to shoulder the burdens of home and family
(Berk 1979; Hoffman and Nye 1974), a factor that may cause them to participate less fully in the labor force. Husbands, on the other hand, seem to
feel less oriented toward family life and more concerned with their career
development. Some researchers have suggested that the financial responsibilities men currently feel toward their families may be at least partially
responsible for this gender-based and possibly destructive orientation
(Myers 1979; Aronson 1973). If these responsibilities were to shift, men
might become more involved in family matters, freeing women to participate more fully in the labor force. Indeed, some evidence suggests that such
an effect does follow (Statham and Larrick 1980; Hudis 1976; Treiman and
Terrell 1975). If changing attitudes toward women's roles do free men from
their traditional labor-force orientation, individuals of both sexes may
come to feel freer to pursue their own personal interests, choosing a mix
that is desirable for each of them regardless of their sex.

Notes

1. The questions were worded as follows: "Now I'd like your opinion
about women working. People have different ideas about whether married

women should work. Here are three statements about a married women with children between the ages of 6 and 12. In each case, how do you feel about such a woman taking a full-time job outside the home: (a) if it is absolutely necessary to make ends meet; (b) if she wants to work and her husband agrees; (c) if she wants to work, even if her husband does not particularly like the idea.'' Respondents were asked if they thought it was definitely all right, probably all right, probably not all right, definitely not all right, or if they were undecided or had no opinion. The responses were coded from five points for ''definitely all right'' to one point for ''definitely not all right,'' and the scale consisted of the sum of these three scores. High scores are thus considered modern, or *nontraditional,* answers.

2. The precise wording of the men's 1967 measure was as follows: ''Now I'd like your opinion about something. People have different ideas about whether married women with children between the ages of 6 and 12 should work. I am going to read five statements. Please select the one statement that best describes your feelings about her taking a full-time job outside the home. (1) she should never work, (2) it is O.K. only if it is absolutely necessary to make ends meet, (3) it is O.K. if the family would like the extra income, (4) it is O.K. if she prefers to work, and (5) she should work.'' These items were scored from one to five with high scores nontraditional.

3. The women were asked how their husbands felt about their working (if they were employed) or their going to work (if they were not employed). They were asked if their husbands (would) (1) dislike it very much, (2) dislike it somewhat, (3) not care either way, (4) like it somewhat, or (5) like it very much.

4. A measure of work experience since leaving school was available for these women but it involved too much missing data to be used with this relatively small sample.

5. In all cases, the mean was substituted for missing data, though we had very few missing cases on any of the variables.

6. Figure 5-3 presents standardized regression coefficients. Complete regression equations for all models in this chapter are available on request from the Center for Human Resource Research.

7. Unreported analyses showed the patterns found in these correlations to be very similar by race. Both races showed equal propensities for agreement between spouses and for wives to accurately perceive their husbands' feelings though this latter tendency was somewhat greater for white couples.

6

Economic Consequences of Poor Health in Mature Women

Thomas N. Chirikos and
Gilbert Nestel

The economic consequences of poor health appear to be more severe for women than for men of the same age. Women are more likely than men to report being work disabled; they also report more severe levels of work disability (Levitan and Taggart 1977). Even if they remain in the labor force, women reduce their working hours more drastically and experience more unemployment in response to health conditions than do men with the same conditions (Waldron 1980). Luft (1975) finds that they also face some reduction in wage rates, thus compounding earnings loss. Women are less likely, however, to receive vocational rehabilitation services and, when they do, are less likely than men to be successfully rehabilitated (Greenblum 1977). They are also less likely to receive disability payments but more likely than men to leave the labor force when they are beneficiaries (Better et al. 1979).

At first glance, these differences might appear to be accounted for by the persistent finding of a sex differential in morbidity or sickness rates. Despite their longer life expectancy, women report substantially more acute and chronic health conditions and more medical-care visits than men of the same age (Verbrugge 1976). But these reported differences probably stem more from socioenvironmental factors and data-collection problems than from biologically based variations in health levels (Nathanson 1975 and 1978); they do not provide a convincing explanation of the differential economic effects of poor health.

An alternative explanation is that the male-female health differential reflects labor-market discrimination against women. Although this possibility is less easily rejected, it cannot be supported without controlling for all other variations in socioeconomic status. Health, like labor-market success, is highly correlated with socioeconomic characteristics such as educational attainment, marital status, and family income. We anticipate that health levels and socioeconomic factors interact to produce markedly different outcomes among individuals of the same sex and age who have similar health problems.

We wish to acknowledge the research assistance of Jeannette Fraser in the preparation of this chapter.

93

This chapter uses the detailed health-related data collected from all respondents for the first time in the 1977 survey to investigate the relationship between women's health and labor-market outcomes. The economic effects of variations in respondent's health status are analyzed from two related perspectives: first, the impact of poor health on labor supply and wage rates is examined in order to compute earnings losses. Second, the analysis is extended to the family unit in order to learn how the woman's health status influences the work behavior and earnings of her spouse.

Health Levels of Mature Women

Measuring Health

Studies of the socioeconomic effects of poor health depend on selection or construction of a suitable measure of health status. Early studies generally relied on questionable health measures that tended to overstate the economic impact of poor health (Chirikos and Nestel 1981). Because health status should be described objectively and measured independently of the behavior it is supposed to explain, subjective evaluations such as self-ratings of the respondent's health as excellent, good, fair, or poor are invalid. For the same reason, behavioral measures such as self-reports of a "work limiting" health problem to indicate variations in health also are ruled out. Measures of functional limitations or impairment status, although far from ideal, are relatively robust indicators of health status. Survey responses about difficulties in physical and psychological functioning (that is, difficulties in walking, stooping, reaching, dealing with people, and the presence of certain signs and symptoms such as weakness, fainting spells and the like) are likely to be more comparable across sample members and more independent of current labor-market activities than the subjective or behavioral alternatives.

We draw on data collected in the 1977 NLS survey to construct an impairment variable. These data are based on responses to thirteen activity limitation questions and eight questions about signs and symptoms. Because incorporating these responses directly into the analysis is cumbersome and leads to ambiguous statistical results, a single index was developed that measures the severity of the respondent's impairment.[1] The index ranges between 0.705 and 5.476, with the lower value indicating no impairment (that is, good health) and the higher value the most severe level of measured impairment. These index values appear in continuous form in the multivariate analysis below, but in the tabular presentations women are categorized according to the severity of their impairments.

Overview of Impairment Status

A substantial proportion of respondents in the 1977 survey reported limitations in physical and psychological functions. About one in two respondents reported one impairment, and one in three reported at least two. Table 6-1 sets out for whites and blacks the prevalence rates of activity limitations by type and severity and the prevalence rates for various signs and symptoms. The most frequently reported difficulties were musculoskeletal limitations, such as ability to lift heavy objects, stand for long periods of time, stoop, and use stairs. A smaller number of women reported having more consequential impairments such as loss of sight, hearing, or ability to deal with people. The prevalence rates for signs and symptoms also were fairly low. Because black rates are roughly double those of whites both for activity limitations and signs and symptoms, the descriptive and multivariate statistical analyses are done separately by race.

Table 6-2 shows that 16 percent of white women are substantially or severely impaired, and close to double that percent of black women are similarly impaired.[2] Approximately equal percentages of white and black women are classified as unimpaired. Table 6-2 also summarizes responses to health-related questions in NLS surveys over the period 1967-1977 by current impairment status. Note initially that impairment status does not account fully for behavior attributed to poor health by the respondent. For instance, between 3 and 5 percent of women classified as having only minor or moderate levels of impairment report that poor health prevents them from working and one in five of these women report that a health problem limits the amount or kind of work they can do.

Current impairment status tends to be closely related to past health. Table 6-2 shows, for instance, that a large proportion of respondents classified as unimpaired in 1977 were (under the various definitions of health encompassed by the data set) in continuous good health over the decade.[3] Interestingly, only about 20 percent of the women classified as substantially or severly impaired in 1977 were in continuous poor health over this period, and the remainder incurred some change in their health status within the decade. Judging by the responses to the 1977 question whether the respondent's health has changed over the past five years, most of the change probably represents deterioration in health status.

Not unexpectedly, demographic and socioeconomic characteristics of women appear to be related to the severity of their impairments. Table 6-3 suggests that the most severely impaired tend to be slightly older and less well educated; they tend to reside in the South; and they are less frequently married. If married, they are more likely to have spouses working in lower-status occupations and their spouses are also substantially more likely to

Table 6-1
Prevalence and Severity of Impairments, by Type of Impairment, 1977

Type of Impairment	Whites[a]		Blacks[b]	
	Prevalence	Percent Severe[c]	Prevalence	Percent Severe[c]
Activity limitations				
Walking	9	7	19	9
Using stairs or inclines	11	12	22	15
Standing for long periods of time	18	24	24	29
Sitting for long periods	11	20	12	26
Stooping, kneeling, or crouching	15	16	22	26
Lifting or carrying weights up to 10 pounds	9	29	16	33
Lifting or carrying heavy weights	26	43	27	52
Reaching	7	20	12	23
Using hands and fingers	6	16	10	17
Seeing (even with glasses)	7	13	12	17
Hearing	5	17	6	28
Dealing with people	3	30	5	35
Other	1	62	2	75
Signs and symptoms				
Pain	2	d	2	d
Tiring easily, no energy	13	d	18	d
Weakness, lack of strength	8	d	15	d
Aches, swelling, sick feeling	10	d	21	d
Fainting spells, dizziness	4	d	13	d
Nervousness, tension, anxiety, depression	15	d	26	d
Shortness of breath, trouble breathing	8	d	14	d
Other	1	d	1	d

[a]2,835 respondents.

[b]1,072 respondents

[c]Proportion of impaired respondents having limitation indicating complete loss of functional capacity.

[d]Question not asked.

have a work-limiting health problem. The more severely impaired tend to hold (or have held) lower-paying and lower-status jobs. Racial differences also appear between labor-market behavior and impairment status, but these may be accounted for by other influences.

Impairments and Labor-Market Outcomes

Reduction in Earnings

We performed a series of multivariate analyses to measure the impact of impairment status on a respondent's earnings. Earnings losses were computed

Table 6-2
Health Status 1967-1977, by Impairment Category, 1977
(percentage distributions)

Impairment Category	Whites				Blacks			
Characteristic	None	Minor or Moderate	Substantial or Severe	Total	None	Minor or Moderate	Substantial or Severe	Total
Health prevents work, 1977	1	3	44	8	1	5	53	16
Health limits work, 1977	2	21	39	14	3	21	30	15
Health does not affect work, 1977	97	76	17	78	96	74	17	69
Total percent	100	100	100	100	100	100	100	100
Continuous good health, 1967-1977	85	57	10	65	75	48	10	52
Continuous poor health, 1967-1977	0	2	22	4	1	2	20	6
Health condition varied, 1967-1977	15	41	68	31	24	50	70	42
Total percent	100	100	100	100	100	100	100	100
Health improved, 1972-1977	9	13	8	10	7	11	9	8
Health deteriorated, 1972-1977	4	17	59	16	4	15	55	21
Health unchanged, 1972-1977	87	70	33	74	89	74	36	71
Total percent	100	100	100	100	100	100	100	100
Sample size	1,495	886	454	2,835	513	251	308	1,072
Total distribution	53	31	16	100	50	22	28	100

Table 6-3
Selected Socioeconomic Characteristics, by Impairment Category, 1977

Impairment Category	Whites				Blacks			
Characteristic	None	Minor or Moderate	Substantial or Severe	Total	None	Minor or Moderate	Substantial or Severe	Total
Age (years)	47	47	49	47	47	47	49	47
Years of schooling	12	12	10	12	12	11	9	11
Non-South (percent)	73	75	64	72	43	39	39	41
Married (percent)	82	82	77	82	61	60	50	58
Occupational status[a]	47	46	39	46	41	34	28	36
Husband's occupational status[b]	42	43	38	42	32	28	28	30
Husband's health limits work (percent)	13	21	38	19	16	28	39	24
In labor force (percent)	69	61	30	60	80	73	32	65
Employed (percent)	66	59	27	58	77	65	29	61
Average wage (dollars)	4.43	4.11	3.49	4.26	4.11	3.79	3.28	3.94
Sample size	1,495	886	454	2,835	513	251	308	1,072
Total distribution	53	31	16	100	50	22	28	100

[a]Mean Bose index score.
[b]Mean Duncan index score.

by combining the net effects of impairment on annual hours worked and on wages. We first used probit analysis to estimate the effects of women's impairment status on the probability that they would be working or seeking work (table 6–4).

As anticipated, we find that women reduce their labor-force participation in response to increasingly severe levels of impairment. To illustrate, the probability that the average white woman without an impairment will be in the labor force is about 60 percent.[4] This probability is reduced by roughly 12 percentage points if she is moderately impaired, 24 percentage points if she is substantially impaired, and about 57 percentage points if she is severely impaired. For black respondents, starting at a 66 percent prob-

Table 6–4
Labor-Force Participation, (ln) Wage and Annual Hours Worked Equations
(t or asymptotic t-ratios in parentheses)

Independent Variables	Participation[a]		(ln) Wage[b]		Hours[c]	
	Coefficient	t ratio	Coefficient	t ratio	Coefficient	t ratio
White Women						
Divorced	0.503**	(3.83)	0.152**	(3.02)		
Separated	0.208	(0.98)	0.042	(0.49)		
Widowed	0.245†	(1.80)	0.022	(0.40)		
Never married	0.324†	(1.82)	0.112	(1.89)		
0–8 years of schooling	−0.337**	(−3.25)	−0.207**	(−3.53)		
9–11 years of schooling	−0.063	(−0.77)	−0.079*	(−2.02)		
13–15 years of schooling	0.123	(1.34)	0.169**	(4.53)		
16+ years of schooling	0.183†	(1.72)	0.306**	(7.84)		
Training, no completion	0.642**	(5.20)	0.142**	(2.57)		
Training, completed	0.580**	(8.51)	0.223**	(6.06)		
Non-South	0.033	(0.52)	0.059*	(2.15)		
Blue collar			−0.097**	(−2.64)		
Child less than 6 years	−0.451**	(−2.67)			−444*	(−2.33)
Other family income	−0.024	(−8.83)			−20**	(−8.14)
Lambda			0.338**	(3.51)		
Predicted (ln) wage					2,453**	(25.49)
Tenure			0.012**	(6.10)		
Full time			0.137**	(4.06)		
Work experience			0.011**	(5.84)		
Impairment index	−0.702**	(−12.65)	−0.230**	(−4.10)	−118	(−1.58)
Constant	1.117**	(11.16)	5.394**	(79.71)	−12,679**	(−22.05)
Sample size	2,279		938		1,725	
R^2 adj			0.326			
Mean dependent variable	0.606		5.988		1,036	

Table 6-4 continued

Independent Variables	Participation[a]		(ln) Wage[b]		Hours[c]	
	Coefficient	t ratio	Coefficient	t ratio	Coefficient	t ratio
Black Women						
Divorced	0.371*	(2.22)	0.016	(0.25)		
Separated	−0.034	(−0.24)	0.007	(0.12)		
Widowed	0.011	(0.07)	−0.097*	(−1.80)		
Never married	−0.093	(−0.46)	−0.102	(−1.31)		
0–8 years of schooling	−0.181	(−1.36)	−0.213**	(−3.44)		
9–11 years of schooling	−0.125	(−1.01)	−0.069	(−1.39)		
13–15 years of schooling	0.326	(1.44)	0.186*	(2.43)		
16+ years of schooling	0.781*	(2.18)	0.549**	(7.29)		
Training, no completion	0.271†	(1.75)	0.142*	(2.08)		
Training, completed	0.684**	(5.01)	0.151*	(2.23)		
Non-South	−0.250*	(−2.31)	0.331**	(6.87)		
Blue collar			0.095*	(2.00)		
Child less than 6 years	−0.325	(−1.61)			−386*	(−1.79)
Other family income	−0.011*	(−2.37)			−13**	(−3.13)
Lambda			−0.170	(−0.83)		
Predicted (ln) wage					1,319**	(8.79)
Tenure			0.003	(0.92)		
Full time			0.116*	(2.34)		
Work experience			0.002	(0.93)		
Impairment index	−0.741**	(−11.30)	0.083	(0.85)	−1,023	(−13.01)
Constant	1.267**	(8.82)	5.468**	(65.14)	−5,665**	(−6.53)
Sample size	888		381		702	
R^2 adj			0.499			
Mean dependent variable	0.611		5.837		1,047	

[a]Probit estimates.
[b]Ordinary least squares estimates.
[c]Tobit estimates.
**Significant at the .01 level.
*Significant at the .05 level.
†Significant at the .10 level.

bability of being in the labor force with no health problems, the corresponding reductions are 12, 25, and 62 percentage points, respectively. The impact of substantial impairments on the labor-force participation of white women is roughly equivalent to their having preschool age children at home. Impairment status is unquestionably the single most important factor in reducing the labor-force participation of black women.

Impairment effects on women's wage rates vary by race (table 6-4).[5] The wage rates of impaired white women are significantly below those of the unimpaired. The wages of the moderately impaired are about 10 percent lower than the unimpaired and about 20 percent lower for the substantially impaired. However, impairment does not appear to have a statistically significant influence on the wages of black women.[6] This finding may stem, however, from occupational segregation and discrimination in female labor markets, especially for black workers. Both conditions would create difficulty in adjusting to health problems through job reassignment and occupational mobility.

Controlling for the influence of (predicted) wages and family characteristics, we find that increases in impairment level also reduce annual hours worked.[7] The reduction is more pronounced for blacks than for whites (table 6-4). The estimate for black women, for instance, translates to average differences (from the unimpaired) of roughly 250 fewer annual hours for the moderately impaired and 1,000 fewer hours for the severely impaired. The reduction in hours for white women, however, is barely at the margin of statistical significance and somewhat smaller in magnitude. It translates to net differences of 166 and 756 fewer annual hours for the moderately and severely impaired, respectively, compared with the unimpaired. These calculations are conditional on the women being in the labor force; in effect, they represent the reduction in hours of impaired women who continue to work. The unconditional or total effect of impairment on annual hours worked is only slightly more than double the conditional effect. Thus women are almost as likely to withdraw from the labor force as to reduce hours of work. Despite the difference in magnitude of reductions in hours worked, the odds of dropping out of the labor force are roughly the same for both white and black women.

To calculate the loss in earnings stemming from the impairment effects on annual hours worked, a dollar value was assigned to the time lost from market work according to the respondent's prospective wage rate.[8] Our estimates of impairment effects on annual hours and wages for working women imply that the average white respondent who is moderately impaired will have earnings reduced by about 20 percent and by almost 80 percent if she is severely impaired. Black respondents incur smaller average earnings reductions; the corresponding declines for the average black woman who is moderately or severely impaired are 14 and 58 percent, respectively. These racial differences are probably understated because blacks, unlike whites, do not face reductions in prospective wages at higher levels of impairment. Consequently, the value of their substantially greater reduction in annual hours is understated relative to whites. For instance, a recalculation of black earnings losses for different levels of impairment at the wage rate of the (average) unimpaired black respondent shows reductions of 17 and 67 percent (respectively) for the moderately and severely impaired, which are very close to the estimates for white women.

Effects on Family Earnings

The economic consequences of the woman's poor health have been examined thus far without any evaluation of their further impact on her spouse's work behavior. To the extent that spouse's hours of work (and hence earnings) are sensitive to wife's health (Parsons 1977), the earnings of the family are necessarily altered.

The impact of impairment status of married women on the annual hours worked by husbands was estimated for married (spouse present) respondents in 1977. Since this relationship may be confounded by the health status of the spouse, we controlled for husband's health and selected other socioeconomic characteristics. Unfortunately, the spouse's impairment index was unavailable; instead, the respondent's report of whether her spouse had a work-limiting health problem was used. We found that while husbands' own poor health significantly reduces their market time (627 hours for whites and 932 hours for blacks), the impairment status of their wives has no statistically significant effect.[9] Although these effects are weaker than expected, they imply that the earnings-loss estimates presented earlier do not necessarily understate the economic consequences of women's poor health on family welfare.

We also tested the relationship of women's health status and their husbands' labor supply with data from a unique subset of families, the almost three hundred respondents in the 1977 NLS Survey of Mature Women whose husbands were also interviewed in the 1976 NLS Survey of Older Men. Because we had previously assigned impairment indexes for these men (Chirikos and Nestel 1981), health levels of both husbands and wives can be represented by comparable measures. Our findings here differ somewhat from those obtained on the full sample of married respondents. We continue to observe (as expected) that a husband's impairment level reduces his average hours of work, but we now also find in black families that a women's impairment influences her husband's labor supply. While the hours of work of white husbands are unrelated to the health of their wives, black husbands appear to increase annual work hours as their wives' impairment level increases. We estimate, for instance, that black husbands of moderately impaired women work roughly sixty hours more each year than husbands of unimpaired women. Even though women's work experience is controlled for, this compensatory behavior may reflect the greater importance of their economic activity in black households.[10]

Conclusions

Women with health problems suffer economic consequences that compound their already disadvantaged position in the labor market. Black women are more likely than whites to suffer substantial or severe impairments—28 percent as opposed to 16 percent. Compared to women with no impairments, those who are impaired have fewer years of school completed and are less likely to be married. Married impaired women are also more likely to have husbands with lower-than-average occupational status and these men are themselves more likely to suffer health problems. Thus deteriorating health significantly increases the distress of the poor.

Even after controlling for socioeconomic status, we find that impairments reduce economic well-being to a significant degree. A moderately impaired woman who is average in every respect and continues to work will earn one-fifth less than an identically situated woman who is unimpaired. Severely impaired women at work lose about two-thirds of their earnings. In contrast to the whites, the losses of black women are influenced more by reductions in market time than in wages. These economic losses understate the total impact because many women in poor health drop out of the labor force.

Notes

1. The statistical findings of Berkowitz and Johnson (1974) and Fechter (1978) illustrate the difficulties of using functional limitation responses as separate regressors. The methods used to construct the impairment index are described in appendix 6A.

2. The values of the impairment index are categorized as follows: .705 = no impairment; .706–.989 = minor impairment; .990–1.275 = moderate impairment; 1.276–1.845 = substantial impairment; 1.846–5.476 = severe impairment.

3. The relevant questions are of two types: self-rating of health status from the 1967 survey, and responses to work limitation questions asked in the 1967, 1972, and 1977 surveys. Respondents who rated their health as excellent to good in 1967 and never reported a work-limiting health problem were considered to be in continuous good health over the decade; respondents rating their 1967 health as fair to poor and reporting a work limitation in each of the three surveys were considered in continuous poor health over the period. All others were considered to have incurred some change in health over the decade.

4. The impact of impairment status was estimated by evaluating the probit equation shown in table 6–4 at the midpoints of the impairment categories as defined in note 2. The case illustrated is for a married woman living in the non-South with twelve years of schooling, with average (other) family income, no training and no preschool children.

5. Following the procedure suggested by Heckman (1980), we correct for the possibility that the potential wages of women who are out of the

work force differ from those of working women by including the estimated labor-force probability as an independent variable in the (ln) wage equation for working women. The sign and magnitude of the estimated coefficient of this variable (lambda) measures the degree of sample selectivity bias. Predicted (ln) wage rates for all members of the cross section are then calculated from this "corrected" (ln) wage equation and included in the annual hours worked equation.

6. Since these estimates are net of the probability of being in the labor force, we can be reasonably confident that they are not affected by the composition of the sample, that is, women employed as wage-and-salary earners at any time between the 1976 and 1977 surveys.

7. Estimating the relationship between impairment and hours of work also commands more complicated treatment. The use of ordinary least squares (OLS) estimation produces estimates with undesirable statistical properties because of the clustering of sample values at zero hours of work. A maximum likelihood approach (*Tobit*) overcomes some of these problems and was used.

Preliminary equations incorporated an interaction term between impairment and occupational assignment to test whether impairment imposes different penalties on individuals performing different job functions. We also tested whether the hours-impairment relationship is confounded by the personal and environmental factors shaping an individual's perception that her health problem is serious enough to warrant changing work behavior. The determinants of self-reported work-limiting health problems and the hours decision were treated as joint or simultaneous choices. However, these more complex models did not shed additional light on the impairment-labor supply relationship and are not presented here.

The expected hours (h_j^*) for women who were working during the survey year and in impairment category I_j is calculated by:

$$h_j^* = \sum_i \beta_i X_i + \beta_j I_j + \hat{\sigma}\frac{f(z)}{F(z)}$$

See McDonald and Moffit (1980) for this derivation and further discussion of the uses of Tobit analysis.

Black women were assumed to have no preschool children at home and average values for other family income and expected wages. Similar assumptions were made for white women except their expected wages varied with their impairment status category.

8. These computations are based on the products of expected wage rates (OLS wage equations) and expected annual hours (from the Tobit hours equations) evaluated for the different impairment categories, I_j. The

expected wages are for married women living in the non-South with twelve years of schooling and eighteen years of prior work experience who were at work in white-collar jobs for employers for whom they had worked an average of nine years.

9. Complete equations showing the effects of husbands' and wives' health status on husbands' annual hours worked are available from the Center for Human Resource Research.

10. Such behavior means that the earnings-loss figure overstates slightly the impact of black women's health on their family's earnings. The impact is nonetheless marginal enough to be ignored for present purposes.

Appendix 6A:
Construction of the
Impairment Index

The large number of impairment items and the need to quantify the health status of the respondent led to a principal components analysis of the impairment data. The solution vector, more specifically its components, was then used as the weights to aggregate the reported impairments and obtain an impairment index value. Linear indexes of health-related items have been used by Grossman and Benham (1974) and by Nagi (1976); we have also constructed such variables in our earlier work (Chirikos and Nestel 1981). In all cases, weights for the linear aggregation of items were obtained by statistical techniques. For instance, Grossman and Benham used principal components analysis to weight self-rated health status and number of symptoms to obtain an index of ill health. Nagi used factor analysis to transform functional limitation items that are quite similar to those used in this study to obtain indexes of physical and emotional performance.

The data used in constructing the index consist of twelve activity limitation questions and seven questions relating to the signs and symptoms of other types of health problems. (The residual "other" categories in both sets of questions were excluded for this purpose.) The presence or absence of the activity limitations was requested from each respondent as well as an indication of the severity of that condition. The battery of questions on signs and symptoms asked for only a dichotomous response; that is, the presence or absence of the symptom was reported, with no indication of its severity. Bivariate contingency tables were prepared for each pair of impairments and a measure of the degree of association computed. The Gamma statistic, rather than the more traditional Pearsonian r, was selected as the summary measure for two reasons: first, because the impairment responses are ordinal in nature and, second, because concern has been expressed in the literature about using ordinal level data in principal components analysis unless the measure of the degree of association is appropriate to the type of response reported. The Gamma coefficients were then arrayed in a square matrix and analyzed by principal components. (The Gamma matrix is available from the authors upon request.) After the initial components were extracted, they were Varimax rotated, providing orthogonal components (factors) as the terminal solution. The resulting component weights measure the amount of residual variance in each component explained by that variable.

Impairment index weights were calculated from the factor estimate matrix. The component scores associated with the highest loading component on each variable were included. The elements of the index are then formed as the product of the matrix of rotated component scores (p_i) and responses to the impairment items, the latter standardized to have zero means and unit variances

$$\sum_{i=1}^{19} p_i I\hat{M}P_i$$

where $I\hat{M}P$ are the normalized responses. A constant of 1.0 was added to each standardized value in the data set so that the range of values for each index would be positive.

The indexing is simply a means for reducing or transforming the data in linear fashion. The transformed data tell us little more than they do in their original form; they are just organized or arranged in a way that facilitates their use. Nonetheless, the results seem plausible from a substantive viewpoint because they reflect both the underlying epidemiological relationships and the rough (rank) ordering of the severity of the impairment items.

7 Economic Consequences of Midlife Change in Marital Status

Gilbert Nestel,
Jacqueline Mercier, and
Lois B. Shaw

The end of marriage leaves most women to face the emotional trauma of the loss of a spouse, the problems of heading a family alone, and the adjustment to the loss of a major source of income. For some middle-aged women this change in marital status comes after they have spent many years as full-time homemakers with little or no experience in the paid labor force. Others have had work experience only in low-paid jobs that are inadequate to support a family. Even women who are well established in the labor market usually suffer a reduction in living standards when the family loses one earner.[1]

Since different potential sources of income, both private and public, may be available depending on the reason the marriage ended, the subsequent welfare of women and their families may be variously affected by widowhood, separation, and divorce. Among midlife women, divorce is becoming increasingly common. Between 1971 and 1976, the number of divorced women heading families increased by 50 percent and the number of separated women by 12 percent, while the number of widows actually decreased slightly (U.S. Bureau of the Census 1972b, 1977).[2] Most previous research has focused on female heads of household as a group, but in order to anticipate future social needs it is important to look separately at the adjustment process for women whose marriages end differently. This chapter compares the consequences for women of widowhood, separation, and divorce: if women in these groups differ in their earnings potential, family responsibilities, and probability of remarrying, their needs for such publicly supported programs as job retraining or public assistance may differ as well.

The authors wish to thank Tania Ramalho for her able research assistance.

Profile of the Women before Their Marriages Ended

Since we want to observe their economic circumstances before their marriages ended, only women who were married and living with their husbands in 1967 are included in this study. The women are classified as widowed, separated, or divorced according to the first reported change in marital status after 1967. The only exception is that women who divorced one survey year after reporting a separation are classified as divorced. Women who remained married continuously to the same spouse between 1967 and 1977 serve as a comparison group.

Table 7-1 provides a profile of these women and their spouses in the survey year preceding the disruption of their marriages.[3] Significant racial differences appear in the likelihood that a woman would be with her 1967 spouse continuously throughout the decade. Almost one in three black women and more than one in seven white women left their 1967 spouses by 1976.[4] The reasons for the changes in marital status also differed between the races. Black women, for example, were twice as likely as whites to become widowed and over three times as likely to separate. The proportion of marriages that ended in divorce (about one in fifteen) was similar for the two racial groups, however.

Since they were younger than the widows, white women who divorced were considerably more likely than those who became widowed to have a preschool child at home and the most likely of the white women to have children under age 18 living in the household. Somewhat different patterns were found in black households, however: black women who subsequently divorced were the least likely group to have a preschool child at home and about as likely as those who ultimately separated to have a child under 18 years in the household. Black women who divorced also had the smallest family size, although black households were generally larger in size than comparably defined white units and more likely to have preschool and school-aged children living at home.

The educational attainments of women who subsequently divorced were higher on average than those of women who separated or became widowed. Women who later divorced were also the most likely to be consistently attached to the paid labor force and, as a consequence, they had the highest average hourly and annual earnings. Here again substantial differences appeared between the racial groups. Black women generally had greater historical and current attachments to the work force but earned considerably less than their white counterparts. The one exception was that, among women who divorced, black women had higher average earnings than white women. On all measures of ability to become self-supporting, the widowed and separated women of both races were not as well off as divorced women.

White women whose marriages were about to end were about as well-

Table 7-1
Characteristics of Married Women and Spouses, by Marital History 1967-1976

Characteristics	Whites					Blacks				
	No Change	Marriage Ended			Total	No Change	Marriage Ended			Total
		Divorced	Widowed	Separated			Divorced	Widowed	Separated	
Demographic, Personal										
Age (respondent)	39	39	44	41	40	40	39	42	38	40
Years married	18	17	21	17	18	18	14	19	16	18
Family size	4.8	4.6	3.8	4.4	4.7	5.6	5.2	5.5	6.5	5.7
Child under 6 years (percent)	31	21	14	24	29	33	17	21	32	31
Child under 18 years (percent)	87	87	69	81	86	79	84	70	85	79
Years of school completed (respondent)	12	12	11	11	12	10	11	9	10	10
Work Experience										
Percent of years worked since marriage	33	43	38	35	34	51	56	47	50	51
Labor-force participation	44.7	68.0	50.8	55.4	47.0	64.4	78.5	62.4	66.9	65.6
Income Measures										
Hourly earnings[a]	3.80	4.11	3.64	3.78	3.82	3.30	4.35	2.18	2.72	3.23
Earnings (respondents)[a]	3,000	4,400	3,000	3,500	3,100	3,400	5,500	1,700	2,400	3,300
Earnings (spouse)[a]	14,100	13,200	9,800	12,800	13,800	9,100	11,300	5,600	6,400	8,600
Family income[a]	20,400	21,100	18,200	18,400	20,300	14,200	19,000	9,600	11,500	13,800
Family income per member[a]	4,700	5,200	5,500	4,600	4,800	3,300	4,700	2,300	2,100	3,200
Percent in poverty	4	8	10	10	5	24	15	48	37	27
Total percent	84.3	7.1	5.2	3.4	100	68.3	6.5	10.7	14.5	100
Sample size	2,010	164	120	79	2,371	453	41	70	94	658

Note: In the survey year preceding the year of the termination of the 1967 marriage. For continuously married women 1971 was used.
[a]1977 dollars.

off economically as women in continuing marriages. The somewhat smaller earnings of husbands whose marriages were about to end were offset either by the wives' higher earnings or by smaller family size, thus making income per family member equal to or even greater than that in continuing families. However, these averages concealed the fact that more families who were about to experience dissolution lived in poverty than continuing intact families.

Divorce among blacks appears to be confined largely to middle-class families. Black women who were nearing divorce were much better off economically than women who would become widowed or separated or even women who would remain married. Prior to the end of their marriages, only 15 percent of those about to divorce were already poor, compared with over 35 percent of women who were about to be separated and nearly half of those about to become widows.

Thus the different groups of women whose marriages were about to end differed in prior work experience, educational attainment, family structure, and economic status. Widows and separated women had less education and work experience than divorced women. Except for black divorced women, black women were at a considerable disadvantage compared with whites. The very high incidence of poverty among black women even before they were separated or widowed suggests that these women face even greater economic hardships after their marriages end.

Consequences of the Loss of a Spouse for Women Who Do Not Remarry

Short-run Changes

Table 7-2 compares labor-market experiences and economic circumstances before and after the end of the marriage for women who do not remarry. Changes in work behavior and economic well-being of these women and their families are shown over a period of three or four years surrounding the change in marital status.[5]

White women (whether widowed, separated, or divorced) increased their participation in the labor force by at least 10 percentage points within one survey date after their marriages ended. Widowed and divorced women had further small increases in participation by the second survey after the marital dissolution. By this time about 85 percent of divorced women were in the labor force, while only 65 percent of widows and 60 percent of separated women were working or looking for work.

Black women who divorced, like their counterparts, increased their labor-force participation in the period directly after the termination of their

Table 7-2
Comparison of Labor-Market and Economic Status before and after the End of Marriage for Women Who Did Not Remarry, by Reason 1967 Marriage Ended

Characteristics	Divorced[a]				Widowed				Separated			
	Survey Year			Sample Size[b]	Survey Year			Sample Size[b]	Survey Year			Sample Size[b]
	Before	After			Before	After			Before	After		
		First	Second			First	Second			First	Second	
Whites												
Labor-force participation	68.1	81.5	84.9	126	50.5	60.3	65.4	105	54.0	65.0	58.6	54
Hourly earnings[c]	4.08	3.99	3.85	99	3.64	3.31	2.62	60	3.97	3.92	4.06	34
Annual earnings[c]	4,400	5,500	6,600	125	3,000	4,100	3,900	103	3,400	4,100	5,800	52
Family income (dollars)[c]	20,900	9,600	10,500	100	18,200	11,600	10,600	75	19,200	8,700	9,300	37
Family size	4.7	3.1	2.9	126	3.8	2.8	2.7	105	4.5	3.2	2.9	54
percent in poverty	10	25	18	100	10	22	17	75	10	43	34	37
Blacks												
Labor-force participation	81.0	92.5	89.7	33	63.3	44.7	53.2	63	66.3	62.6	56.5	77
Hourly earnings[c]	4.51	4.33	4.72	25	2.16	3.21	3.06	32	2.71	3.03	3.69	50
Annual earnings[c]	5,900	6,600	7,900	33	1,800	1,700	2,200	63	2,500	3,800	3,000	75
Family income[c]	20,500	10,300	12,300	26	9,800	6,000	6,000	45	11,800	9,200	7,600	57
Family size	5.0	3.8	3.6	33	5.5	4.1	4.1	63	6.6	5.3	5.4	77
Percent in poverty	8	30	9	26	48	65	70	45	41	45	61	57

Note: The comparison is restricted to women who did not remarry within two survey periods after the end of their 1967 marriages.
[a]Women who divorced by the survey year following a separation are classified as divorced.
[b]The smallest number of respondents in the three reference periods.
[c]1977 dollars.

marriages. In contrast, black widowed women showed a sharp decline in participation in the period immediately after the end of the marriage. At each interview after separation, the participation of separated women declined as well. Apparently the very low wages that black separated women and widows could command did not allow them to support their families in any event, and the small amounts they could earn did not compensate for the strain of being both breadwinners and homemakers.

Contrasting patterns also appeared in average hourly earnings among the different groups of women. The mean hourly earnings either declined or remained the same in all of the white subgroups and among the black divorcees, suggesting that the new entrants into the labor force earned, on average, less than those who were already working. Separated and widowed black women showed some improvement in hourly earnings over time, perhaps reflecting both increased earnings of continuing workers and the fact that the workers with the lowest pay left the labor force. Family income was substantially lower after the disruption than during the marriage: income was cut in half for white separated women and divorced women of both races, with smaller decreases among other groups. Since average family size declined by only slightly more than one person, economic well-being was substantially reduced. These data illustrate the importance of the husband's earnings to family income. Despite their increases in labor-force participation, the women's rather modest increase in annual earnings could by no means compensate for the loss of the earnings of their spouses.

Increases in poverty appeared among all groups, especially severely for black women who were widowed or separated. Both of these family types had a very high incidence of poverty even when the husband was living in the household, and after the marriage ended the percent in poverty increased from 40 to 60 percent among separated women and from 50 to 70 percent among widows.

Sources of Income

How do women whose marriages end compensate for the loss of their husband's earnings? To answer this question, we shift to a somewhat longer range perspective and compare the sources of family income in 1966 and 1976 for women who had not remarried by 1977 (table 7–3).[6] Before their marriages ended, husband's earnings amounted to between 70 and 80 percent of total family income in white families; the lower figure was for families in which the husband died within the following decade and may reflect his poor health. White wives made modest contributions amounting to 15–18 percent of total income. Among black families, husbands contributed a smaller percentage of total income and wives' contributions were correspondingly larger, reaching 37 percent of the total for black women who later divorced.

Table 7-3
Sources of Family Income in 1966 and 1976 among Women Who Did Not Remarry, by Reason 1967 Marriage Ended
(percentage distributions)

Source	1966			1976		
	Divorced	*Widowed*	*Separated*	*Divorced*	*Widowed*	*Separated*
Whites						
Earnings (respondent)	15	18	17	71	50	a
Earnings (spouse)	80	72	76	0	0	a
Earnings (other family members)	22	4	3	11	13	a
Social Security benefits	0	0	0	1	20	a
Public assistance[b]	0	0	1	2	1	a
Other transfer payments[c]	1	5	3	1	8	a
Alimony and child support	1	0	1	7	0	a
Other income[d]	1	1	1	7	8	a
Total percent	100	100	100	100	100	a
Total family income (mean)	18.700	16,700	15,800	11,800	11.500	a
Sample size	67	78	27	63	60	16
Blacks						
Earnings (respondent)	37	21	24	57	39	27
Earnings (spouse)	53	62	68	0	0	0
Earnings (other family members)	2	5	1	35	20	8
Social Security benefits	1	3	1	0	22	4
Public assistance[b]	4	2	5	6	12	53
Other transfer payments[c]	3	5	0	2	7	3
Alimony and child support	0	0	0	1	0	0
Other income[d]	1	1	0	0	1	5
Total percent	100	100	100	100	100	100
Total family income (mean)	16,600	10,200	10,200	13,000	8,400	6,200
Sample size	24	47	39	24	45	33

[a]Percentage not shown when sample size less than 20.
[b]Includes AFDC and food-stamp benefits.
[c]Includes unemployment compensation, disability income, and income from pensions. Also includes Title V benefits in 1966.
[d]Includes interest, dividend, and rental income.

Significant racial and marital status differences also appeared in sources of income and their relative importance after the end of a marriage. The earnings of divorced and widowed women of both races became the major source of their family's income, while for black separated women public assistance was the most important source. In black families, especially among the widowed and divorced, other family members' earnings made an important contribution to family income. Although it was less important in white families, the average amount contributed by other family members (usually children) was actually greater than the amount received from alimony and child-support payments.[7]

Public-transfer payments were an important source of income for the families of widowed and separated women. Over half of the income in families of black separated women came from public-assistance payments, and black widows also received about one-fifth of their income from this source. For both races one-fifth of the income in families of widows came from Social Security survivor's benefits. Both Aid to Families with Dependent Children (AFDC), the most common kind of public assistance, and Social Security survivor's benefits are payable only while there are children at home.[8] Thus many widows and women who are separated will face the loss of a major source of income between the time when their children are grown and age 60 (or 62) when they become eligible for Social Security benefits, either as widows or on their own account.

Determinants of Remarriage

Up to this point we have examined the economic effects of marital disruption for women who do not remarry. For some women who lose a spouse, remarriage will eventually lead to resumption of the economic status that was lost through divorce or widowhood. If women who are least able to become self-supporting are most likely to remarry, the economic consequence of the increasing rates of divorce among women at midlife will be less severe than otherwise. The economic theory of marriage predicts that the least economically independent are the most likely to marry (Becker 1974). Support for the *independence effect* of a woman's earnings potential has been found in research on remarriage (Thornton 1977; Glick 1980; Becker, Landes, and Michael 1977).[9] The receipt of public-assistance income has also been shown to deter remarriage (Bahr 1979). However, Mott and Moore (1981) found no evidence of an independence effect on the remarriage probabilities of young women.

The effect of children on the likelihood of remarriage is not clear-cut. On the one hand, a larger family will be more difficult to support, making remarriage attractive for women. On the other hand, men may be less willing to marry women with children. Research on this issue has produced mixed results. Thornton (1977) found that children inhibit remarriage, while Koo and Suchindran (1980) found that this effect holds only for women below age 25, that children have no effect at ages 25-34, and that beyond age 35, children increase the likelihood of remarriage. Remarriage is also more likely for women who lose their spouses while in their thirties than for women whose marriages end at older ages, reflecting the increasing ratio of unmarried females to unmarried males as age increases.

We use multiple classification analysis here to determine what factors influenced remarriage.[10] Explanatory variables include education and work experience (which make self-support more feasible), other income available, age, and presence of children at home. We also control for length of time since the end of the marriage, health, and whether the respondent lived in a metropolitan area. The number of previous marriages and attitudes toward women's roles are included as variables that may reflect tastes for conventional homemaker roles. Since remarriage rates have been found to be lower for black women than for white (Farley and Hermalin 1971), race is also included as a control variable. Divorced and widowed women are analyzed separately to test whether behavioral relationships are different for these groups. The sample consists of women who were married in 1967 and whose marriages ended by divorce or death of spouse by 1976.[11]

Overall, about one-third of the divorcées, but only one-sixth of the widows, had remarried by 1977 (table 7-4). White women who were divorced were much more likely to remarry than were black women: less than 10 percent of black divorced women but over 35 percent of white divorced women had remarried by 1977. The difference in remarriage rates between widows of the two races was much smaller and not statistically significant.

For widows there is some support for the hypothesis that the independence effect, as measured by education and work experience after widowhood, deters remarriage. Women who had attended college were less likely to remarry than those who had only a high-school education or less. In addition, widows who were working at the time of the last interview before their husband's death had less than half the remarriage probability of women who were not working. However, neither the number of years of work experience before they were widowed, the other income available to them, nor whether they had children affected the remarriage probabilities of widows.

Among divorced women, evidence for the independence effect is mixed. Neither recent labor-force participation nor the amount of work experience before the divorce affected the chances of remarrying. While women who did not complete high school were more likely to remarry than those with more education, the difference between the groups does not

Table 7-4
Probability of Remarriage among Divorced Women and Widows,
1967-1977: Multiple Classification Analysis Results

Characteristics	Divorced Women		Widows	
	Adjusted Percentage Remarrying[a]	Sample Size	Adjusted Percentage Remarrying[a]	Sample Size
Race	**			
Whites	36.8	162	17.0	115
Blacks	7.8	43	9.4	67
Years of school completed				
Less than 12 years	41.3	71	16.9	104
12	31.6	91	18.4	63
13 years or more	30.1	42	2.8	15
Health				
Affects work	33.2	38	15.0	47
Does not affect work	34.6	167	17.1	133
Age when marriage ended	**		**	
30–39	45.8	88	37.2	34
40–44	28.5	65	14.1	65
45–54	15.4	49	9.1	80
Children under 18 years				
None	43.8	35	12.7	48
One or more	32.6	163	17.1	128
NA	b	7	b	6
Residence	**		†	
In SMSA	26.0	104	20.3	86
Not in SMSA	43.0	101	12.2	96
Labor-force participation			**	
In labor force	34.8	132	8.0	72
Not in labor force	33.6	73	21.9	110
Percent of years worked since school				
Less than 25 percent	28.7	48	19.9	46
25–49	37.2	53	15.2	50
50–74	38.6	38	16.1	40
75 or more	33.5	44	19.9	27
NA	32.0	22	5.7	19
Other family income	**			
Less than $1,000	27.1	102	17.5	75
$1,000–$4,999	20.1	31	10.9	24
$5,000 or more	57.6	37	15.5	46
NA	42.0	35	16.6	37
Number of previous marriages			**	
One	34.0	142	11.2	143
Two or more	35.2	63	36.3	38
Role attitude	**		**	
Traditional	51.5	47	28.7	61
Intermediate	33.7	112	11.6	85
Nontraditional	18.3	45	33.4	31

Table 7-4 continued

	Divorced Women		Widows	
Characteristics	Adjusted Percentage Remarrying[a]	Sample Size	Adjusted Percentage Remarrying[a]	Sample Size
Months since marriage ended	**		*	
1–23	17.7	40	5.5	30
24–47	26.5	44	12.4	48
48–71	37.9	40	27.0	24
72–95	36.5	54	17.0	39
96 or more	68.3	25	22.6	40
Total sample	34.3	205	16.0	182
$\bar{R}^2$ (adjusted)	.317		.226	

[a]Predicted percentage marrying after controlling for all other variables in the model.
[b]Percentage not shown when sample size less than 15.
**Significant at .01 level.
*Significant at .05 level.
†Significant at .10 level.

reach statistical significance. However, when attitutes toward women's roles were excluded from the analysis (results not shown), the effect of education did become significant. It is not clear whether the effect of education on remarriage is due to the greater economic independence that education makes possible or to less traditional attitudes toward women's roles, which are correlated with education. In any event, more traditional women were considerably more likely to remarry than were less traditional women. Women with more income from sources other than their own earnings were also more likely to remarry than those with less income, contrary to the independence hypothesis. In addition, the presence of children, which might suggest greater need, did not affect remarriage probabilities.

Among widows, the relationship between attitudes and remarriage was more complex than among divorced women. Women with both very traditional and very modern attitudes were more likely to remarry than were women whose attitudes were intermediate. Widows who had been married more than once were also much more likely to marry than those with only one marriage; remarriage was as common for these widows as for their divorced counterparts.

The probability of remarriage declined markedly with age for both divorced women and widows in the sample. Nearly half of women whose divorce occurred before age 40 had remarried by 1977, while only 15 percent of those who divorced after age 45 had remarried. At each age, widows were less likely to remarry; their rates of remarriage declined with age from nearly 40 to less than 10 percent. The fact that there are more unmarried females than males at older ages may make the independence effect less important as women grow older. Some women who would prefer to remarry may not have an opportunity to do so.[12]

Other influences on remarriage included place of residence, health, and the length of time since the marriage had ended. Widows with health problems and those living outside metropolitan areas were less likely to remarry. However, divorced women were more likely to remarry if they lived outside metropolitan areas. The reason for this difference is not apparent. At each length of time since marriage, divorced women were more likely to remarry than widows, even after controlling for the effect of age.[13]

Even if they are less likely to remarry than divorced women, we do find that among widows, those who have the greatest economic need are most likely to remarry. Among divorced women this result is less certain. Women with the least education are most likely to remarry, but this may be due in part to their generally more traditional attitudes toward women's proper roles. Although there is some evidence for an independence effect, especially among widows, it cannot be assumed that those least able to support themselves will in fact remarry. The probability of remarriage falls dramatically with age; many women whose marriages end at midlife cannot expect to remarry.

The Economic Consequences of Marital-Status Changes over Ten Years

To sum up the effects of marital-status changes over time, figure 7-1 shows average family income at the beginning and ending of the ten-year period for women who lost a spouse and did not remarry compared with women who remarried and women who remained continuously married throughout the period.[14] All groups of women whose marriages ended and who did not remarry between 1967 and 1977 had lower incomes in the latter year than the former. White women who did not remarry had income losses of over 35 percent (all figures are in 1977 dollars). Black separated women had the most drastically reduced income, 40 percent lower than ten years earlier, when their incomes had already been below those of most other groups. In contrast, continuously married women of both races had increases in income of about 30 percent over the ten years. Women who remarried showed an increase of only 18 percent, somewhat below that of continuously married women.

The decline in income among women whose marriages ended during the ten years overstates the family's loss in economic status, since family sizes

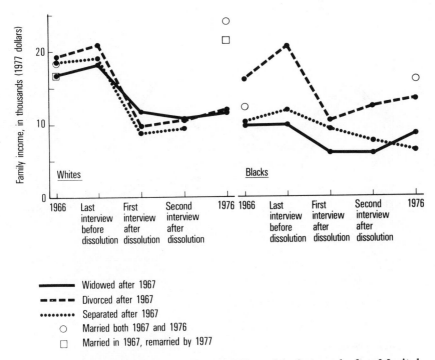

Figure 7-1. Family Income in 1966, 1976, and before and after Marital Dissolution

were also declining. In figure 7-2 economic well-being is measured by the *poverty ratio;* that is, the ratio of family income to poverty-level income. Since the calculation of poverty-level income takes family size and residence into account, the poverty ratio shows the amount by which a family's income exceeds or falls short of its basic level of needs.[15]

It can be seen that the decreases in income for women whose marriages ended during the decade were on average offset by decreases in family size, leaving most groups about as well-off at the end of the decade as they were at the beginning. An exception is black separated women, who were definitely worse off in 1976. The extreme situation of these women is highlighted by these data: they were already the poorest of married women in 1966, and by 1976 their average income was below the poverty line. In fact, over three-quarters of these families were poor.

While these figures suggest that, except for black separated women, many female-headed families eventually regain their former level of economic well-being, this conclusion should be tempered by several consid-

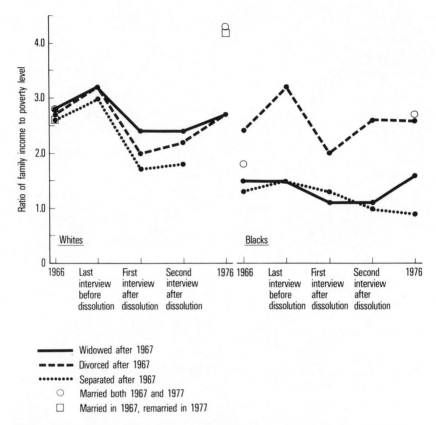

Figure 7-2. Ratio of Family Income to Poverty-Level Income in 1966, 1976, and before and after Marital Dissolution

erations. First, as figure 7-2 shows, the use of 1966 as the base date for comparison understates the economic loss from marital dissolution; women did not regain the peak level of economic well-being they enjoyed just before their marriages ended. Second, it is partly the decrease in family size as children leave home that increases the standard of living of the remaining family members. Thus, the period of reduced living standards shown in figure 7-2 by the dip in the poverty ratio usually coincided with the childhood and adolescence of young family members, with possible adverse effects on their educational attainment and future prospects.[16] Finally, the economic picture for all female-headed families is one of relative deprivation compared with that of husband-wife families. For those women who remained married and those who remarried, economic well-being improved over the decade while for female-headed families economic well-being remained constant. Relative to their married friends, unmarried women became relatively worse off over the ten years.

Conclusions

Women at midlife who head families differ considerably in their ability to provide adequate economic support for themselves and their children. The incidence of poverty was far higher for both white and black female heads than for their married counterparts. In both races, separated women were worst off economically: by 1977 three-quarters of black separated women were poor. White women in all groups and divorced black women increased their labor-force participation following marital disruption but black separated women and widows worked less. High percentages of both groups were poor even while married. Since these women could not earn enough to support themselves and the two or three children they had, many became at least partially dependent on public transfers. Widows usually received Social Security survivors benefits; separated women received welfare.

Women who lose their husbands at midlife are apt to spend quite long periods as heads of households, and many will never remarry. Only one-third of divorced women and one-sixth of the widows in the sample had remarried by 1977. Even after six or more years from the end of their marriages, about one-half of divorced women but only one-quarter of widows had remarried. Remarriage was somewhat more likely among those who were worse off economically and those with little education. However, black women and older women were less likely to remarry regardless of their economic needs.

About 15 percent of both white and black divorced women who did not remarry received added formal education between 1967 and 1977, as did 6 percent of the widows and 8 percent of the separated women. However, as previously shown (table 7-1), these divorced women already had more education than widowed or separated women. Therefore, those women who especially needed further education and training were the least likely to receive it.

The incidence of poverty among older female family heads is cause for concern. Women who are now receiving Social Security survivors benefits or AFDC will lose this income when their children leave home. If by that time they are not established in the labor market, it may be more difficult for them to find and keep jobs as they grow older. With ten to twenty-five years to go until the usual retirement age, many will find self-support difficult.

Notes

1. The loss of income and high risk of becoming poor following the end of marriage has been well documented through research using longitudinal data. See, for example, Mott (1979), Shaw (1978), Hampton, (1975), Hoffman (1977), Corcoran (1979a), and Mott and Moore (1978).

2. These increases are for women aged 35–64. At the youngest end of the age range, 35–44, the number of divorced women increased by two-thirds in five years, even though the number of women in this age range was actually declining.

3. The comparison data for women who were married throughout the 1967–1977 period is for 1971, the approximate midpoint for the data reported for the women whose marriages ended.

4. In order to have two interviews after the end of the marriage, only marriages ending prior to the 1976 interview are considered here.

5. Interviews were at intervals of one or two years. The time between the last interview before and the second interview after the marriage ended was either three or four years.

6. Since income information is asked in less detail on telephone interviews, it is not possible to do a detailed analysis of income sources in all years. Therefore, these sources were investigated in the calendar year preceding the 1967 and 1977 surveys.

7. It should be stressed that for some of the sample these adjustments have occurred after as many as eight years. Child-support payments are known to be higher in the earliest years after divorce.

8. Food stamps are the only source of public-transfer income available to nonaged persons without children. Severely disabled persons may also be eligible for Supplementary Security Income (SSI).

9. Research on marital dissolution has also found that women with higher earnings potential are more likely to divorce (Ross and Sawhill 1975; Cherlin 1978).

10. This technique required that all factors be categorized but does not assume a linear association between each factor and the probability of remarriage. The constant term of the relationship is constrained to be the mean of the dependent variable. All observations are weighted by the inverse of their sampling fractions.

11. Women whose marriages ended in separation are excluded from the analysis unless their separation was followed by a divorce or the death of the spouse. Thus women who return to their spouse after a period of separation and those who remain separated are deleted from the sample of women eligible for remarriage.

12. At ages 30–34, the number of unmarried men and women was approximately equal in 1976; at ages 35–44, the ratio of unmarried women to

men was 1.3 to 1; while at ages 45–54 it was 1.65 to 1. At ages 55–64 there are twice as many unmarried women as men (U.S. Bureau of the Census 1978, p. 39).

13. Even if twenty-four months were added to the time since dissolution for divorced women on the grounds that divorce is often preceded by separation and in any event takes some time to secure, the remarriage rates of divorced women are still higher than those of widows at each length of time except 48–71 months.

14. Fewer than fifteen black remarried women remained in the sample and reported their family incomes in 1976. Therefore, figures for black remarried women are not shown. Similarly the number of white separated women was too small for reliability in the final year.

15. For example, low family income during the high-school years substantially increases the probability of dropping out of school (Shaw 1982).

16. Poverty-level income for each family size and a description of the poverty-level concept may be found in Current Population Surveys. See, for example, U.S. Bureau of the Census (1972a).

8

Summary and Conclusions

Lois B. Shaw

When today's middle-aged women were growing up, returning to the labor force after childrearing was not usual for white women, and the opportunities black women had were mainly limited to domestic service and agriculture. Many of the whites were not prepared for the world of work, which the majority nonetheless have entered. Those black women with high-school or college educations have enjoyed an expansion of opportunities in white-collar jobs, but a majority of this generation of black women did not finish high school and have not shared these opportunities.

Although many did not plan ahead for working after their children went to school, and few received adequate training for occupations now in demand, some women have prepared for new roles and occupations by returning to school or seeking additional training. Chapter 1 showed that between 1967 and 1977, 7 percent of white and 10 percent of black middle-aged women completed at least one additional year of formal schooling, while about 18 percent of both races completed other training courses and use their new skills on their jobs. These gains in education and work-related skills were spread unevenly across the population. In general those with the most previous education were most likely to undertake further education or training—nearly 20 percent of white women and 30 percent of black women who had attended college prior to 1967 returned for additional education between 1967 and 1977, and even more received other kinds of job training. About 10 percent of high-school dropouts also returned to school, many of them completing work for a high-school diploma; but among the least educated—those who had never attended high school—less than 5 percent received either job training or additional schooling. Thus those who most needed additional skills to obtain good jobs were the least likely to participate in the quite impressive upgrading of skills undertaken by this generation of women at midlife.

Ten years of information on the same women give us a unique opportunity to see how women manage work and family responsibilities over time. During the ten-year period, over 80 percent of white women and 90 percent of black women worked at some time. The variety of work patterns is striking: about 30 percent of white women worked fairly continuously; about one-third were reentrants or intermittent workers; and about 20 percent had

127

worked at some time during these ten years but were no longer employed in the last year of the interviews. About 40 percent of black women worked for most of the period, one-quarter were intermittent workers or, less commonly, reentrants, and another quarter had left employment.

Chapters 2 and 3 focused on the problems of reentrants and women who worked intermittently. The worsening economic climate of the middle 1970s damaged the work prospects of both groups. Reentrants who lived in areas of high unemployment ran an increased risk of leaving the labor force again after reentry. Those who reentered the labor force during the middle 1970s after an absence of at least five years had wages nearly 10 percent lower in real terms than the wages of women who had entered in the late sixties or early seventies, but neither the length of time since they had last worked nor the fact that they were somewhat older than women who entered earlier explained their lower wages. One possible explanation is that the slow growth of the economy combined with the influx of young women workers from the baby-boom generation brought increased competition for entry-level jobs that did not require much work experience.

Middle-aged women work intermittently for a variety of reasons. Family constraints still interrupt work and women—blacks in particular—increasingly leave jobs because of health problems. However, economic conditions also affect their work patterns: 25–30 percent of intermittent workers gave business conditions as reasons for leaving their jobs. In addition, about 15 percent of white and 25 percent of black women who worked intermittently were unemployed for more than thirteen weeks during the years 1971–1977. Women's contributions to family income are often important to family welfare, and their lack of steady work may cause hardship.

In chapter 1 we found that white women who worked fairly continuously had real wage gains of about 13 percent and black women had gains of 17 percent between 1967 and 1977. In addition, there was an increase in professional and managerial jobs: among the continuously employed of both races, 30 percent of whites and nearly a quarter of blacks worked in these occupations by 1977.

On the other hand, there was very little movement out of jobs that traditionally have been considered women's work. As chapter 4 shows, many of these jobs are low paid, particularly outside the white-collar occupations. This study found no support for the widely held view that women choose stereotypically female occupations because these jobs do not require continuous work experience and are well suited for women who plan interrupted work careers. Women who have the most continuous work experience are just as likely to be in female-typed jobs as are women who spent many years out of the labor force. Much of the sex segregation of occupations may be attributable to employer discrimination when women apply for jobs thought to be more appropriate for men, to women's perceptions that they will encounter discrimination and, in some cases, to their own preferences for jobs they see as appropriately feminine.

During the ten years of these NLS interviews, women's proper role in society was the subject of much debate. The questioning of women's roles and the changing views on the subject have had an impact on women in their middle years as well as younger women. Between the years of 1972 and 1977, the percentage of women who agreed that a woman's place is in the home fell from 45 to 32 percent. The importance of these changing views for the working lives of both women and men is the subject of chapter 5, which uses information from interviews with husbands and wives who were both surveyed by the NLS. Women with nontraditional attitudes were found to work more than those with traditional attitudes. Moreover, there appears to be some feedback from work experience to attitudes both for the women themselves and their husbands: if their wives work outside the home, men's attitudes toward women's roles become less traditional. While the husbands' expressed attitudes had no effects on their wives' work, women's perceptions of their husbands' attitudes were very important. Men's attitudes toward women's roles affect their own work as well: those with less traditional attitudes worked less than more traditional men. It may be that less traditional men are more likely to share breadwinner and home roles with their wives. Some men may retire early or take time away from work to make midlife career changes if they do not feel that they must be the sole support of their families. Although these results apply to men who are entering or near to retirement, they may portend more general flexibility in roles for both men and women in the future.

Chapter 6 investigated health problems of middle-aged women and the effect of health on work activity. An index of health impairment was constructed using questions on specific impairments such as difficulties in hearing, lifting, or climbing steps and such symptoms as pain and dizziness. The incidence of all such impairments was higher for black women than for white: 16 percent of white women and 28 percent of black were judged to be substantially impaired.

In chapter 3 health problems were identified as one of the major causes for working irregularly or dropping out of the labor force, especially for black women, and chapter 6 confirms that health problems affect women's work. White women, whose wages were generally higher to begin with, suffered larger wage losses than black women from a given degree of impairment, but black women were more likely to leave the labor force or reduce their hours of work. Among those who continued to work despite a moderate degree of impairment, earnings losses from lower wages and time lost from work averaged about 20 percent of predicted annual earnings for both races; the substantially impaired lost more than half of their earnings. The consequences of earnings losses are particularly severe for women who head households and for families in which the wife formerly contributed substantially to family income, a not uncommon situation, especially among black families.

Female heads of household, both white and black, have a much higher risk of poverty than their married counterparts. While 4 percent of white and 16 percent of black married women were poor in 1977, the corresponding percentages for unmarried women were 18 and 41 percent. Chapter 7 examined the varied circumstances that follow divorce, separation, and widowhood at midlife. Some women whose marriages ended during the 1967–1977 period were able eventually to regain their former level of economic well-being because their earnings increased and needs decreased as children grew up and left the home or began to contribute to family income. Some women remarried, but as they reach ages when unmarried women increasingly outnumber unmarried men, remarriage becomes less likely. Although women who were less able to support themselves were somewhat more likely to remarry, age was an important deterrent. Black women also were less likely to remarry than their white counterparts. Most women who are widowed or divorced at midlife will be heads of household for considerable periods; many will never remarry. With fifteen to twenty-five years before retirement age, those who have little work experience may need additional training if they are to become self-supporting.

Black women who are not married at midlife are one of the most disadvantaged groups in society. During the 1975–1976 recession, they experienced much more unemployment than other women their age. They are more likely to suffer from poor health than their married counterparts. Most black separated women and widows have low levels of education and have not shared in the improved job opportunities and higher wages experienced by better-educated black women. With poor job prospects, many have left the labor force and depend on Social Security survivors benefits or welfare, but they will lose these sources of income when their children are grown.

Policy Implications

The economic downturn of the midseventies appears to have made it more difficult for middle-aged women to establish themselves in the labor force. Competition with younger women for entry-level jobs may have exacerbated the employment problems of both groups. Cuts in public spending on education, health, and social services in the 1980s will not only reduce the human capital of current and future generations; these cuts also contribute to the employment problems of middle-aged women, who often work in these fields and who encounter more difficulties than their younger counterparts when they must make occupational changes. Many women will be unable to become self-supporting or make contributions to family income unless a societal commitment is made to a sufficient level of economic growth to provide jobs for all.

The risks of becoming poor following divorce, separation, or widowhood were highlighted in chapter 7. Many middle-aged women who are currently married will be widowed before reaching retirement age and the husbands of others will become disabled and unable to support their families. For some of these women who are not now working or who work only sporadically at poorly paid jobs, additional education and training could improve their chances of escaping poverty both now and in old age. Currently, federal and state displaced-homemaker programs reach only a few women in this situation. While some women are too close to retirement age to make retraining feasible, those who have a decade or more of potential working life ahead should have access to job-training programs and, if necessary, financial support while they are trained. Counseling about different kinds of work available in local communities would help women to choose occupations that are in demand and allow some women to train for better-paid nontraditional jobs. At the local level, community organizations could do more to provide after-school childcare and supervised activities for teenagers; such programs, as well as benefiting children, would allow female heads of household the flexibility to accept a wider variety of jobs.

Health becomes a problem for increasing numbers of women as they grow older. Probably as a consequence of their low economic status both in childhood and as adults, middle-aged black women especially have a high incidence of health problems. Some of these women who were formerly in jobs requiring heavy physical labor have been unable to continue working, and counseling and retraining for less physically demanding jobs might allow them to be reemployed. Others, especially those who are severely disabled or have little education, probably cannot become self-supporting, but society has an obligation to provide support for these victims of old injustices.

As they approach old age, problems of adequate health insurance and pension coverage will become more important for the current generation of middle-aged women. Many women who work intermittently or in low-paid jobs have neither health insurance nor pensions through their own employment. Affordable health insurance for persons not covered on their own or their spouses' jobs is an important goal for older women. With their intermittent work records, many women never acquire pensions of their own, and many private pension plans offer little or no protection for survivors, especially if the husband dies before reaching retirement age. Some state and federal pension systems also provide inadequately for survivors. It is not clear to what extent legislation can require private pensions to cover workers after short periods of employment or provide survivor benefits without discouraging employers from offering pensions at all. This issue needs further study. The lack of other sources of pension income for many women highlights the importance of adequately financing the Social Security system, which will be the principal source of income for many women during old age.

Most of the policy implications already mentioned point to the importance of steady, adequately paid employment for the economic welfare of many women and their families. The policies recommended for middle-aged and older women tend to be remedial. For the future, it is important that younger women recognize the likelihood that they will need to be employed and to prepare for jobs that will allow them to be self-supporting. Guidance counsellors at the high-school level need to encourage young women to consider nontraditional jobs with higher pay than traditional female jobs and to take the mathematics, science, or shop courses that will give them flexibility in their later choices. Enforcement of antidiscrimination legislation also remains important in achieving broader access to high quality education and well-paid jobs.

Women's Work Now and in the Future

The important contributions that many women make to their families' economic well-being has been a recurring theme of this book. Chapter 1 showed that 50 percent more husband-wife families would be in poverty if the wives did not work. Families above the poverty line often depend on women's earnings to help children attend college or achieve middle-class standards of living. For the 20 percent of women who are unmarried at midlife, employment is even more crucial, since the majority support themselves largely through their own earnings. Clearly many families are able to participate in the mainstream of American life through the contributions of working women.

While this book has concentrated on women's paid employment, their work in the home should not be forgotten. For the majority of women in the sample, childrearing, homemaking, and providing support for husbands' careers was a full-time job for many years and remains a second job when they return to paid employment. The fact that this work is not included in Gross National Product has the unfortunate effect of blinding us to its importance to the nation's economy.

For the most part, the paid work of today's middle-aged women has resembled their work at home: they are most commonly employed in occupations where they provide services for others, whether in the helping professions such as teaching and nursing, in service work such as cleaning offices or serving food, or in clerical work, facilitating the record keeping and communication demanded by a complex industrial society. Only a small percentage of midlife women have moved into nontraditional jobs; even fewer are employed in high-paid, prestigious professional and managerial jobs. In the NLS sample there are only three doctors, one lawyer, and five women with other doctoral degrees (except for the doctors, none of these hold high-paid jobs). In 1977 about a dozen women earned $25,000 or more in managerial or sales positions in private industry or government; these represent less than 1 percent of employed women in the sample. Clearly the much-publicized movement of women into high-level jobs has scarcely touched the generation of women who have been the subject of this book.

Has society gained or lost by having women's abilities concentrated in the home and underutilized in the labor market? Many economists would argue that since families chose this division of labor, they must have valued women's work in the home above whatever contribution they could have made in the work force. Yet if women were completely content with their choices, there would be no women's liberation movement, and if nothing more than uncomplicated individual choices were at stake, there would be no profamily backlash. Historian Carl Degler (1980) believes that tension between family and market place has been increasing throughout the two hundred years of American history. Our society values individual achievement, productivity, and efficiency on the one hand but on the other it values the home as a shelter from competitiveness, as a place to find love and appreciation for human qualities not highly valued by a market economy, and as the only proper setting for the nurturing of children. Assigning one set of values and corresponding duties to men and the other to women has been one way of assuring that neither set is completely lost.

Whatever the advantages of this division of labor in the past, it seems clear that at present it leaves women at an economic disadvantage. With rising divorce rates and low pay for women who lack work experience, being a full-time housewife has become a high-risk occupation (Bergmann 1981). At every age after adulthood is reached, women have a 50 percent higher risk of being poor than men. In old age the disparity is even greater as women outlive their husbands and find themselves with inadequate pensions. Partly because of the economic vulnerability of women, children also suffer from a relatively high risk of being poor.[1] Although most women and their children manage to avoid outright poverty, divorce and widowhood often bring sharp decreases in economic well-being to women who have put homes ahead of personal achievement.

Another source of tension between work and family arises because childrearing does not provide a lifelong career. Women are living longer and having fewer children. If a woman has two children and stays at home until they enter school, she will be a full-time housewife for no more than a quarter of her preretirement adult years. Young women who have witnessed their mothers reenter the labor market and have their abilities underutilized in low-paid jobs may be unwilling to sacrifice their own ambitions to this short period of caring for children. Furthermore, some young women aspire to the prestigious, decision-making kinds of jobs that so few women in older generations attained. Many pursue these goals from the same achievement-oriented motives as men; for some, however, the opportunity to contribute a new perspective to the professions and the intellectual life of their time, or to see that women's experiences and interests are represented in politics and the business world, are additional reasons for their dedication to careers.

Whether because of economic necessity, their own aspirations for more rewarding roles, or their awareness of the economic risks of being full-time housewives, increasing numbers of young married women are working outside the home. Yet, among NLS young women in the age range 24 to 34, about 30 percent have not worked as much as six months in any of the five to ten years since their first child was born, over half have spent one or more years at home, and only 12 percent have worked in every year (Mott and Shapiro, forthcoming). While this generation of women may have less trouble reentering the labor market or breaking out of low-paid employment, the problems detailed here for mature women have by no means disappeared. The tension between family and marketplace persists. Going back to traditional family roles will not solve the twin problems of women's economic vulnerability and the underutilization of their abilities when their children are grown. We must find ways to achieve a better balance between home and work for both women and men.

Note

1. While 19 percent of children under age 16 live in poverty, 8 percent of adult males and 12 percent of adult females below age 65 live in households with incomes below the poverty line. Nineteen percent of elderly women and 11 percent of elderly men are poor (U.S. Bureau of the Census 1981, table 20). Although the percentages in absolute poverty are relatively small, many women have incomes that are above the poverty line but still very low compared to those of men.

Bibliography

Albrecht, S.L., H.M. Bohr, and B.A. Chadwick. "Changing Family and Sex Roles: An Assessment of Age Differences." *Journal of Marriage and the Family* 41 (February 1979):41–50.

Araji, S. "Husbands and Wives Attitude-Behavior Congruence on Family Roles." *Journal of Marriage and the Family* 39 (May 1977):309–321.

Aronson, G. "Marriage with a Successful Woman: A Personal Viewpoint." In *Women and Success,* edited by R.B. Kundsin. New York: William Morrow and Company, 1973.

Bahr, S.J. "The Effects of Welfare on Marital Stability and Remarriage." *Journal of Marriage and the Family* 41 (August 1979):553–560.

Becker, G.S. *The Economics of Discrimination.* 2d ed. Chicago: University of Chicago Press, 1971.

Becker, G.S. "A Theory of Marriage: Part II." *Journal of Political Economy* 82 (March/April 1974, part 2):S11–S26.

Becker, G.S., E.M. Landes, and R.T. Michael. "An Economic Analysis of Marital Instability." *Journal of Political Economy* 85 (December 1977):1141–1187.

Beller, A.H. "Occupational Segregation by Sex: Determinants and Changes." Paper presented at the Population Association of America Meetings, Denver, Colorado, 1980.

Bergmann, B.R. "The Economic Risks of Being a Housewife." *American Economic Review* 71 (May 1981):81–86.

Berk, S.F. "Husbands at Home: Organization of the Husband's Household Day." In *Working Women and Families,* edited by K.W. Feinstein. Beverly Hills: Sage Publications, 1979.

Berkowitz, M., and G. Johnson. "Health and Labor Force Participation." *Journal of Human Resources* 9 (Winter 1974):117–128.

Better, S., P. Fine, D. Simison, G. Doss, R. Walls, and D. McLaughlin. "Disability Benefits and Disincentives to Rehabilitation." *Milbank Memorial Fund Quarterly* 57 (Summer 1979):412–427.

Blau, F.D. "The Impact of the Unemployment Rate on Labor Force Entries and Exits." In *Women's Changing Roles at Home and on the Job.* National Commission for Manpower Policy Special Report no. 26, 1978.

Blau, F.D., and W.E. Hendricks. "Occupational Segregation by Sex: Trends and Prospects." *Journal of Human Resources* 14 (Spring 1979):197–210.

135

Borus, M.E., F.L. Mott, and G. Nestel. "Counting Youth: A Comparison of Youth Labor Force Statistics in the Current Population Survey and the National Longitudinal Surveys." In *Conference Report on Youth Unemployment: Its Measurement and Meaning.* U.S. Department of Labor, Washington, D.C.: U.S. Government Printing Office, 1978.

Bowen, W.G., and T. Finegan. *The Economics of Labor Force Participation.* Princeton, N.J.: Princeton University Press, 1969.

Cain, G.G. *Married Women in the Labor Force.* Chicago: University of Chicago Press, 1966.

Center for Human Resource Research. *The National Longitudinal Surveys Handbook.* Columbus: The Ohio State University, revised 1981.

Centers, R., B.H. Raven, and A. Rodrigues. "Conjugal Power Structure: A Re-Examination." *American Sociological Review* 36 (April 1971): 264–278.

Chafe, W.H. *The American Woman.* New York: Oxford University Press, 1972.

Chenoweth, L.C., and E. Maret. "The Career Patterns of Mature American Women." *Sociology of Work and Occupations* 7 (May 1980): 222–251.

Cherlin, A. "Employment, Income, and Family Life: The Case of Marital Dissolution." In *Women's Changing Roles at Home and on the Job.* National Commission for Manpower Policy Special Report no. 26 (September 1978), pp. 157–180.

Chirikos, T., and G. Nestel. "Impairment and Labor Market Outcomes: A Cross Sectional and Longitudinal Analysis." In *Work and Retirement: A Longitudinal Survey of Men,* edited by H. Parnes. Cambridge: MIT Press, 1981.

Cogan, J. "Labor Supply with Costs of Labor Market Entry." In *Female Labor Supply: Theory and Estimation,* edited by J.P. Smith. Princeton, N.J.: Princeton University Press, 1979.

Corcoran, M.E. "The Economic Consequences of Marital Dissolution for Women in the Middle Years." *Sex Roles* 5 (March 1979a):343–353.

Corcoran, M.E. "Work Experience, Labor Force Withdrawals, and Women's Wages: Empirical Results Using the 1976 Panel of Income Dynamics." In *Women in the Labor Market,* edited by C.B. Lloyd, E.S. Andrews, and C.L. Gilroy. New York: Columbia University Press, 1979b.

Cronkite, R.C. "The Determinants of Spouses' Normative Preferences for Family Roles." *Journal of Marriage and the Family* 39 (August 1977): 575–585.

Degler, C.N. *At Odds: Women and the Family in America from the Revolution to the Present.* New York: Oxford University Press, 1980.

Deutsch, H. *Psychology of Women.* New York: Brune and Stratton, 1944.

Dowdall, J.A. "Structural and Attitudinal Factors Associated with Female Labor Force Participation." *Social Science Quarterly* 55 (June 1974): 121-130.

England, P. "Assessing Trends in Occupational Sex Segregation, 1900-1976." In *Sociological Perspectives on Labor Markets,* edited by I. Berg. New York: Academic Press, 1980.

Farley, R. *Growth of the Black Population.* Chicago: Markham, 1970.

Farley, R., and A.I. Hermalin. "Family Stability: A Comparison of Trends Between Blacks and Whites." *American Sociological Review* 36 (February 1971):1-17.

Fechter, A. "Health Conditions and Earnings Capacity: A Human Capital Model." In *Policy Analysis with Social Security Research Files.* U.S. Department of Health, Education and Welfare, Washington, D.C.: U.S. Government Printing Office, 1978.

Ferree, M.M. "Causal Models of Stability and Change in Women's Work Relevant Attitude and Employment Behavior." Final Report for grant from the Employment and Training Administration, U.S. Department of Labor, Storrs, Connecticut, 1979.

Glick, P.C. "Remarriage: Some Recent Changes and Variations." *Journal of Family Issues* 1 (December 1980):455-478.

Grant, J.H., and D.S. Hammermesh. "Labor Market Competition Among Youths, White Women and Others." National Bureau of Economic Research Working Paper no. 519, 1980.

Greenblum, J. "Effect of Vocational Rehabilitation on Employment and Earnings of the Disabled: State Variations." *Social Security Bulletin* 40 (December 1977):3-16.

Griliches, Z. "Wages of Very Young Men." *Journal of Political Economy* 84 (August 1976):S69-S85.

Grossman, M., and L. Benham. "Health, Hours and Wages." In *The Economics of Health and Medical Care,* edited by M. Perlman. New York: Halsted Press, 1974.

Hampton, R. "Marital Disruption: Some Social and Economic Consequences." In *Five Thousand American Families—Patterns of Economic Progress,* edited by G.J. Duncan and J.N. Morgan, vol. 3. Ann Arbor: The Institute for Social Research, University of Michigan, 1975.

Heckman, J.J. "New Evidence on the Dynamics of Female Labor Supply." In *Women in the Labor Market,* edited by C.B. Lloyd, E.S. Andrews, and C.T. Gilroy. New York: Columbia University Press, 1979.

Heckman, J.J. "Sample Selection Bias as Specification Error." In *Female Labor Supply: Theory and Estimation,* edited by J. Smith. Princeton, N.J.: Princeton University Press, 1980.

Heckman, J.J., and R.J. Willis. "A Beta-Logistic Model for the Analysis of Sequential Labor Force Participation by Married Women." *Journal of Political Economy* 85 (February 1977):27–58.

Hoffman, L.W., and F.I. Nye. *Working Mothers.* San Francisco: Jossey-Bass, 1974.

Hoffman, S. "Marital Instability and the Economic Status of Women." *Demography* 14 (February 1977):67–76.

Hudis, P.M. "Commitment to Work and Family: Marital Status Differences in Women's Earnings." *Journal of Marriage and the Family* 38 (May 1976):267–278.

Jusenius, C.L. "The Influence of Work Experience and Typicality of Occupational Assignment on Women's Earnings." In *Dual Careers,* vol. 4. U.S. Department of Labor, Employment and Training Administration, Monograph no. 21, Washington, D.C.: U.S. Government Printing Office, 1976.

Kanter, R.M. *Men and Women of the Corporation.* New York: Basic Books, 1977.

Kim, S., and J.A. Murphy. "Changes in Labor Force and Employment Status." In *Dual Careers,* vol. 2. U.S. Department of Labor, Manpower Administration, Monograph No. 21. Washington, D.C.: U.S. Government Printing Office, 1973.

Koo, H.P., and C.M. Suchindran. "Effects of Children on Women's Remarriage Prospects." *Journal of Family Issues* 1 (December 1980): 497–515.

Kosa, J., and R.E. Coker, Jr. "The Female Physician in Public Health: Conflict and Reconciliation of the Sex and Professional Roles." *Sociology and Social Research* 49 (April 1965):294–305.

Levitan, S., and R. Taggart. *Jobs for the Disabled.* Baltimore: Johns Hopkins Press, 1977.

Long, J.E., and E.B. Jones. "Labor Force Entry and Exit by Married Women: A Longitudinal Analysis." *Review of Economics and Statistics* 62 (February 1980):1–6.

Lundberg, F. and M. Farnham. *Modern Women: The Lost Sex.* New York: Harper and Brothers, 1947.

Luft, H.S. "The Impact of Poor Health on Earnings." *Review of Economics and Statistics* 57 (February 1975):43–57.

Macke, A.S. "The Family and the Occupational World: Linkages and Change." Paper presented at the American Sociological Association Meetings, San Francisco, California, September, 1978.

Macke, A.S., P.M. Hudis, and D. Larrick. "Sex Role Attitudes and Employment Among Women: A Dynamic Model of Continuity and Change." In *Women's Changing Roles at Home and on the Job,* edited by I. Sawhill. National Commission on Manpower Policy, Special Report no. 26, 1978.

Macke, A.S., and W.R. Morgan. "Maternal Employment, Race, and Work

Orientation of High School Girls." *Social Forces* 57 (September 1978): 187-204.

Mason, K., and L.L. Bumpass. "U.S. Women's Sex-Role Ideology, 1970." *American Journal of Sociology* 80 (March 1975):1212-1219.

McDonald, J., and R. Moffitt. "The Uses of Tobit Analysis." *Review of Economics and Statistics* 62 (May 1980):318-321.

McLaughlin, S. "Occupational Sex Identification and the Assessment of Male and Female Earnings Inequality." *American Sociological Review* 43 (December 1978):909-921.

Mincer, J. "Labor Force Participation of Married Women: A Study of Labor Supply." In *Aspects of Labor Economics: A Report of the NBER,* edited by H.G. Lewis. Princeton, N.J.: Princeton University Press, 1962.

Mincer, J., and H. Ofek. "Interrupted Work Careers: Depreciation and Restoration of Human Capital. *Journal of Human Resources* 17 (Winter 1982):3-24.

Mincer, J., and S. Polachek. "Family Investments in Human Capital: Earnings of Women." *Journal of Political Economy* 82 (March/April 1974):S76-S108.

Morgenstern, R.D., and N.S. Barrett. "The Retrospective Bias in Unemployment Reporting by Sex, Race and Age." *Journal of the American Statistical Association* 69 (June 1974):355-357.

Mortimer, J.T., and J. Lorence. "Work Experience and Occupational Value Socialization: A Longitudinal Study." *American Journal of Sociology* 84 (May 1979):1361-1386.

Mott, F.L. *The Socioeconomic Status of Households Headed by Women.* U.S. Department of Labor R & D Monograph 72. Washington, D.C.: U.S. Government Printing Office, 1979.

Mott, F.L., and S.F. Moore. "Marital Disruption: Causes and Consequences." In *Years for Decision,* vol. 4. U.S. Department of Labor R & D Monograph 24. Washington, D.C.: U.S. Government Printing Office, 1978.

Mott, F.L., and S.F. Moore. "Myths and Realities About Remarriage for Young American Women." Paper presented at the Population Association of America Meetings, Washington, D.C., March 1981.

Mott, F.L., and D. Shapiro. "Work and Motherhood: The Dynamics of Labor Force Participation Surrounding the First Birth." In *Years for Decision,* vol. 4. U.S. Department of Labor R & D Monograph 24. Washington, D.C.: U.S. Government Printing Office, 1978.

Mott, F.L., and D. Shapiro. "Continuity of Work Attachment among Young Mothers." In *The Employment Revolution,* edited by F.L. Mott. Cambridge: MIT Press, forthcoming.

Myers, H. *Women at Work: How They're Reshaping America.* Princeton,

N.J.: Dow Jones Books, 1979.

Nagi, S. "Epidemiology of Disability Among Adults in the United States." *Milbank Memorial Fund Quarterly* 54 (Fall 1976):439-467.

Nathanson, C. "Illness and the Feminine Role: A Theoretical Review." *Social Science and Medicine* 9 (1975):57-62.

Nathanson, C. "Sex Roles as Variables in the Interpretation of Morbidity Data: A Methodological Critique." *International Journal of Epidemiology* 7 (September 1978):253-262.

Oppenheimer, V.K. *The Female Labor Force in the United States.* Population Monograph Series, no. 5. Berkeley: University of California, 1970.

Parnes, H.S. "The National Longitudinal Surveys: New Vistas for Labor Market Research." *American Economic Review* 65 (May 1975): 244-249.

Parsons, D.O. "Health, Family Structure, and Labor Supply." *American Economic Review* 67 (September 1977):703-712.

Perrucci, C.C. "Minority Status and the Pursuit of Professional Careers: Women in Science and Engineering." *Social Forces* 49 (September 1970):245-259.

Polachek, S.W. "Occupational Segregation Among Women: Theory, Evidence, and a Prognosis." In *Women in the Labor Market,* edited by C.B. Lloyd, E.S. Andrews, and C.L. Gilroy. New York: Columbia University Press, 1979.

Pullman, T.W. "Parameterizing Age, Period, and Cohort Effects: An Application to U.S. Delinquency Rates, 1964-1973." In *Sociological Methodology,* edited by K.F. Schuessler. Jossey-Bass Publishers, 1978.

Robinson, G.J. "Labor Force Participation Rates of Cohorts of Women in the United States: 1890 to 1979." Paper presented at the Population Association of America Meetings, Denver, Colorado, 1980.

Ross, H.L., and I.V. Sawhill. *Time of Transition: The Growth of Families Headed by Women.* Washington, D.C.: The Urban Institute, 1975.

Rubin, L.B. *Women of a Certain Age.* New York: Harper and Row, 1979.

Sampson, J.M., M.M. Dunsing, and J.L. Hafstrom. "Employment Status of the Wife-Mother: Psychological, Social, and Socioeconomic Influences." *Home Economics Research Journal* 3 (June 1975):266-279.

Sandell, S.H. "The Economics of Family Migration." In *Dual Careers,* edited by H. Parnes, et al., vol. 4. U.S. Department of Labor R & D Monograph 21. Washington, D.C.: Government Printing Office, 1976.

Sandell, S.H., and D. Shapiro. "The Theory of Human Capital and the Earnings of Women: A Reexamination of the Evidence." *Journal of Human Resources* 13 (Winter 1978):103-117.

Scanzoni, J. *Sex Roles, Work and Fertility.* New York: The Free Press, 1977.

Schmidt, P., and R.P. Strauss. "The Prediction of Occupation Using Multiple Logit Models." *International Economic Review* 16 (June 1975): 471–486.

Shapiro, D. and J.E. Crowley. "Aspirations for the Future: Education, Work Activity, and Fertility. In *Pathways to the Future: A Report on the National Longitudinal Survey of Youth Labor Market Experience in 1979,* edited by M.E. Borus. Columbus, Ohio: Center for Human Resource Research, The Ohio State University, 1981.

Shaw, L.B. "The Economic Consequences of Marital Disruption." In *Women's Changing Roles at Home and on the Job.* National Commission for Manpower Policy Special Report no. 26, 1978.

Shaw, L.B. "Changes in the Work Attachment of Married Women, 1966–1976." Paper presented at the annual meeting of the Population Association of America, Denver, Colorado, 1980.

Shaw, L.B. "High School Completion for Young Women: Effects of Low Income and Living With a Single Parent." *Journal of Family Issues* 3 (June 1982):147–163.

Shuval, J.T. "Sex Role Differentiation in the Professions: The Case of Israeli Dentists." *Journal of Health and Social Behavior* 11 (September 1970):236–244.

Spitze, G., and J.L. Spaeth. "Human Capital Investments of Married Female College Graduates." Paper presented at the American Sociological Association Meetings, New York, 1976.

Spitze, G.D., and L.J. Waite. "Young Women's Tastes for Market Work: Responses to Marital Events." In *Research in Population Economics,* edited by J.L. Simon and P.H. Lindert, vol. 3. Greenwich, Conn.: JAI Press, 1981.

Statham, A. "Discreet Identities and Their Outcomes." Paper for The Center for Human Resource Research, Columbus, Ohio: The Ohio State University, 1980.

Statham, A., and D. Larrick. "Perceived Responsibility for the Family's Support and Women's Success." Paper for The Center for Human Resource Research, Columbus, Ohio: The Ohio State University, 1980.

Stephan, P.E., and L.D. Schroeder. "Career Decisions and Labor Force Participation of Married Women." In *Women in the Labor Market,* edited by C.B. Lloyd, E.S. Andrews, and C.L. Gilroy. New York: Columbia University Press, 1979.

Strober, M. "Comment." In *Women in the Labor Market,* edited by C.B. Lloyd, E.S. Andrews, and C.L. Gilroy. New York: Columbia University Press, 1979.

Suter, L.E., and H.P. Miller. "Income Differences Between Men and Career Women." *American Journal of Sociology* 78 (January 1973): 962–975.

Sweet, J. *Women in the Labor Force.* New York: Seminar Press, 1973.

Taylor, P. "Institutional Job Training and Equal Employment Opportunity in Federal Civil Service." Paper presented at the American Sociological Association Meetings, New York, 1980.

Thornton, A. "Decomposing the Remarriage Process." *Population Studies* 31 (July 1977):383-392.

Treiman, D.J., and K. Terrell. "Sex and the Process of Status Attainment: A Comparison of Working Women and Men." *American Sociological Review* 40 (April 1975):174-200.

U.S. Bureau of the Census. *Current Population Reports,* series P-60, no. 86. "Characteristics of the Low Income Population, 1971." Washington, D.C.: U.S. Government Printing Office, 1972a.

U.S. Bureau of the Census. *Household and Family Characteristics: March, 1971,* series P-20, no. 233. Washington, D.C.: U.S. Government Printing Office, 1972b.

U.S. Bureau of the Census. *Household and Family Characteristics: March, 1976,* series P-20, no. 311. Washington, D.C.: U.S. Government Printing Office, 1977.

U.S. Bureau of the Census. *Statistical Abstract of the United States, 1977.* Washington, D.C.: U.S. Government Printing Office, 1978.

U.S. Bureau of the Census. *Current Population Reports,* series P-60, no. 119. "Characteristics of the Population Below the Poverty Level: 1977." Washington, D.C.: U.S. Government Printing Office, 1979.

U.S. Bureau of the Census. *Current Population Reports,* series P-60, no. 127. "Money Income and Poverty Status of Families and Persons in the United States: 1980." Washington, D.C.: U.S. Government Printing Office, 1981.

U.S. Commission on Civil Rights. *Social Indicators of Equality for Minorities and Women.* Washington, D.C.: U.S. Commission on Civil Rights, 1978.

U.S. Department of Labor. *Employment and Earnings,* vol. 26, no. 11. Washington, D.C.: U.S. Government Printing Office, 1979, p. 81.

U.S. Department of Labor. *The Employment and Training Report of the President.* Washington, D.C.: U.S. Government Printing Office, 1980.

Verbrugge, L. "Females and Illness: Recent Trends in Sex Differences in the United States." *Journal of Health and Social Behavior* 17 (December 1976):387-403.

Wachter, M. "A Labor Supply Model for Secondary Workers." *Review of Economics and Statistics* 54 (May 1972):141-151.

Waite, L.J. "Projecting Female Labor Force Participation from Sex-Role Attitudes." In *Women in the Labor Force in 1990,* edited by R.E. Smith. Washington, D.C.: The Urban Institute, 1979.

Waite, L.J., and R. Stolzenberg. "Intended Childbearing and Labor Force Participation of Young Women: Insights From Recursive Models."

American Sociological Review 41 (April 1976):235-252.

Waldron, I. "Employment and Women's Health: An Analysis of Causal Relationships." *International Journal of Health Services* 10 (1980): 435-454.

Winsborough, H.H. "Age, Period, Cohort, and Education Effects on Earnings by Race—An Experiment with a Sequence of Cross Sectional Surveys." In *Social Indicator Models,* edited by K.C. Land and S. Spilerman. New York: Russell Sage, 1975.

Winsborough, H.H., and O.D. Duncan. *Analyzing Longitudinal Data: Age, Period and Cohort Effects.* New York: Academic Press, forthcoming.

Index

About the Contributors

Thomas N. Chirikos is a professor in the Department of Preventive Medicine at The Ohio State University. His areas of research include health economics and health planning in the United States and abroad.

Thomas Daymont is an assistant professor in the Department of Industrial Relations and Organizational Behavior at Temple University. His previous publications and current research efforts deal with a variety of labor-market topics including Equal Employment Opportunity and aging and work.

Jacqueline Mercier was formerly a graduate research associate at the Center for Human Resource Research. She recently completed the M.A. in labor and human resources and is employed as a health-care administrator.

Gilbert Nestel is a research scientist at the Center for Human Resource Research. He has published extensively in the fields of retirement, aging, health, and labor-market problems of older workers.

Theresa O'Brien was formerly a research assistant at the Center for Human Resource Research. She is currently employed as a management consultant.

Patricia Rhoton is data archivist for the National Longitudinal Surveys at the Center for Human Resource Research. She recently received the Ph.D. in sociology from Notre Dame University.

Anne Statham is an assistant professor of sociology at the University of Wisconsin, Parkside. Her research and teaching interests are in the areas of sex roles, the family, and social psychology. She has published extensively on sex-role attitudes and employment, sex-typed teaching styles among university faculty, and the effects of mothers' employment on daughters' work orientation.

About the Editor

Lois Banfill Shaw is a research scientist with the National Longitudinal Surveys at the Center for Human Resource Research, The Ohio State University. She has written extensively on issues concerning women's work and economic status. She received the Ph.D. in economics from the University of Michigan and reentered the labor force while in her forties. In writing about the working lives of middle-aged women she makes use of her experience as both analyst and participant.